RSPB WILD THINGS TO DO WITH WOODLICE

MICHAEL COX

D1146757

A&C Black • London

First published 2010 by
A & C Black Publishers Limited
36 Soho Square, London W1D 3QY

www.acblack.com

ISBN 978·1·4081·2783·4

A CIP catalogue for this book is available from the British Library.

Author: Michael Cox
Illustration: John Kelly
Design: Calcium Creative Ltd and Geoff Ward

This book is produced using paper that is made from wood grown in managed, sustainable forests. It is natural, renewable and recyclable. The logging and manufacturing processes confirm to the environmental regulations of the country of origin.

Printed in China by C&C Offset Printing Co.

Introduction

Forget tedious TV talent shows and soppy soaps! Nature's got the 'X' factor in abundance, surprises by the forest-full and 'wow-power' by the pond-load!

Every day thousands of really wild miracles take place all around us: ants milk greenfly, ugly bugs morph into beautiful beetles, birds build brilliant nests, hares go boxing, and acorns grow into giant oak trees.

In this book you'll discover how to enjoy your very own slice of all this really wild action. In no time at all you'll be mesmerised by moles, hooked on hedgehogs, captivated by caterpillars, gobsmacked by goldfinches, flabbergasted by fieldfares and bedazzled by buzzards and butterflies. And with the appliance of science you'll visit spider websites, watch gruesome insect footage, and create oodles of awesome wildlife photographs with your compact camera or mobile phone.

So, if YOU want to discover …

WHERE to go twitching, twanging, grunting and caterpillar hunting, find brilliant nature screen savers, watch seals cavorting, starlings swarming and otters frolicking.

Or HOW to grow a tomato in a bottle, build a bird hide, make a bee box (or a wasp wrestle), make a triple-decker for a hungry woodpecker, listen to some tawny owls (it's a hoot!), and of course go wild with some woodlice… then this is the book for you.

Contents

Put together your nature enthusiast's backpack

You will need:

- A mobile camera phone or a digital camera – preferably with
  1. zoom settings for shy sparrowhawks, bashful bullfinches and retiring roe deer
  2. macro settings for in-your-face foxgloves, humongous hawk moths and larger-than-life ladybirds
- Bird seed, in case the birds get peckish
- Chocolate, in case you get peckish
- A nature notebook, pen, pencil and pencil sharpener: for making notes and sketches when you go feral in the forest or batty at the beach
- A drink, in case you get thirsty
- An insect net – for bagging bugs
- Some more chocolate (for when the first lot's gone)

- A plastic bottle – to keep your captive bugs in so you can sketch them and snap them, before granting them early release for good behaviour
- Sweets (in case you get fed up with the chocolate)
- Compact binoculars – for spying on stoats, observing owls and keeping tabs on tree creepers
- A plant press – perfect for mummifying mugwort, flattening frogbit and preserving primroses
- A 15 cm ruler – it measures your treasures – this is a really important way of identifying what you've found and adding more info to your sketches
- 5/10 x magnifier – for scrutinizing stag beetles, checking out chickweed and clocking cockroaches (if you're brave enough)
- Specimen collection bags – lots of sealable plastic bags for collecting lovely lichen, fab feathers, oversize owl pellets and brilliant bird nests (but only if they've got VACANT - TO LET signs, of course)

Build a natural den

Take your tame adult and a few pals into the woods and see who can build the most original and weather-proof den out of all the natural materials you find there.

Learn to spot and identify signs of wildlife

When you're out walking in the countryside, look out for signs of local wildlife. These might be nuts nibbled by mice and squirrels, badger fur, fox droppings, owl pellets and tree bark rubbed smooth by deer polishing their antlers.

Go birdwatching. It's in your nature!

Birdwatching should come to you completely naturally.

Human beings have had thousands of years of practice at this sort of thing. In fact, for hundreds and hundreds of generations their very survival depended on remaining camouflaged and completely still in one spot for hour after hour until some unsuspecting deer, rabbit, wild boar (or cheese sandwich) happened to wander by. At which point they would leap out and clobber it senseless, thus ensuring that they and their family had something for dinner that night.

So get yourself into a primitive 'my survival depends on silence, stealth and cunning' frame of mind. You can start by making a bird hide, which will significantly help your stealth (see activity 13, page 12)! However, you must not leap out and clobber the first bird that lands next to your hide, as that would be defeating the object of the exercise (and more to the point, chaffinches and woodpeckers taste really horrible).

Find out what soil's made from

A lot of people would say that soil is *not* dirt. But if you got soil on your hands, you'd say they were *dirty*! So, what actually *is* soil?

To find out, you need some glass jars with screw-top lids, a jug of water and some small soil samples taken from various places, such as your garden, the woods, a sandy area (and that bit behind your ears where you never wash).

WHAT TO DO:

1. Put your samples in the jars.

2. Label them to say where the soil came from. Pour in twice as much water as there is soil.

3. Tightly screw the tops on the jars and shake them. Leave the jars to stand a few minutes then examine them.

   You will now see that some of the contents of your jar have sunk to the bottom. This is the 'mineral' part of the soil – in other words, crushed-up rocks. Above the minerals you'll see a sort of brown soup with 'scum' on top. This is the 'organic' part of the soil, and it's made up of decomposed dead plants and animals, bacteria and lots of other micro-organisms.

So soil is really rocks and dead things, mashed up to form the brown stuff which covers so much of our planet and is absolutely vital to the survival of every living thing. Yes, when living things die, nature recycles them to become a part of new living things. So, at sometime in the future, a bit of *you* could become part of a carrot, or a dragonfly, or even a bit of a human being who isn't born yet!

Wild Tips To Watch Birds

Don't get the wind up

- Check the wind direction by throwing a leaf into the air and seeing which way it floats. If it's blowing from behind you it will blow your scent towards animals and alert them to your presence.

Become completely inhuman!

Try to make your body shape as unlike that of a human being as you possibly can, by crawling, crouching or stooping. And never stand with your hands on your hips when you're birdwatching. You'll just end up looking rather silly.

Dress down

Wear clothes that blend in with your surroundings and don't make a lot of noise by rustling or squeaking.

Brightly coloured clothes are definitely to be avoided.

Avoid clunky loose change in your pockets, or carrying wildlife-watching equipment that rattles and bangs.

Well, your trousers are rather loud

Shhhh!

Resist the temptation to yell out in excitement when you see something really gobsmacking. Also refrain from singing loud opera choruses when stalking creatures or running towards small, timid animals yelling, 'KILL! KILL! KILL!'

Learn all the right moves

- Move smoothly, slowly and silently. Never make sudden movements.
- Avoid stepping on twigs or getting your clothes snagged on vegetation.

Get eagle-eyed

Your eyes are one of the best pieces of nature-watching kit you've got, followed closely by your ears and nose. Train your senses to become aware of unusual movements, shapes, colours and sounds, which may indicate the presence of a creature that is trying to be just as invisible as you are. Your trusty nose will also tell you when you're near 'odiferous' nature, such as a fox's territory or some wild garlic plants.

Do you ever get the feeling we're being watched?

Wild Tips To Watch Birds

How to make a bird hide – Method One

1. Sneak up on it
2. Make a noise
3. Watch the bird fly into a bush or tree

Well done, you've made a bird hide!

How to make a bird hide – Method Two (This a much better one!)

WHAT YOU NEED:

- An old clothes horse (wooden type)
- An old dark-coloured blanket

WHAT TO DO:
Erect the clothes horse then sling the blanket over it. Get inside and wait.

98, 99, 100! – here I come, ready or not!

Disappear under a camouflage net

If you haven't got time to build a hide but want to remain undetected while you watch wildlife, simply sling a blanket over yourself. It's the perfect thing *not* to be seen in!

Check out the rest of the really wild action

Added bonus! Being inside your hide won't only make you invisible to birds, but will also conceal you from all the other things which haunt wild places such as foxes, badgers, deer, stoats, weasels (and pixies). So be prepared to be surprised, amazed and possibly even slightly scared!

Tip number two for bringing out birds

Another way to attract birds is to suck with your lips tight to make a short, sharp kissing noise known as 'chipping'. And if you want to attract tawny owls, try cupping your hands to make an airtight space and blowing between your thumbs.

Try this tip for bringing birds out of cover: Pissssshing!

In summer birds are often hidden by thick foliage. If you want them to pop out from their leafy cover, make a quiet 'pissssh!' sound and the inquisitive little feather-brains won't be able to resist popping out to investigate.

Listen to the spooky
'tap tap tap' of the Death Watch Beetle

These wood-boring beetles live in the rafters and beams of old buildings and make a tapping sound to attract mates. In the bad old days when people sat at the bedsides of their dying loved ones they would hear this spooky 'tap tap tap' sound in the quiet of the night. It became so closely associated with death that on simply seeing one of the beetles, people would regard it as an omen foretelling someone's end. **NB:** If you do happen to hear a death watch beetle tapping away in the dead of night, tell your parents about it. It's eating your house!

Make a nature-print T-shirt

Print your nature photos onto fabric transfer sheets then iron them onto a T-shirt for an item of clothing that's completely unique!

Make a nature-print pillowcase

If you don't want to do a T-shirt print, how about decorating a pillowcase?

Skeletonize a leaf

When you "skeletonize" a leaf you're exposing the veins that it uses to transport food. Tack an old piece of carpet to a board then put a fresh green leaf on it, top-side up.

Now, using an old shoe brush or hairbrush, begin lightly tapping the leaf whilst holding it firmly in place. **NB**: Don't tap too hard or you'll just end up with a load of mush on your brush!

Keep tapping until all the fleshy green part of the leaf is gone whilst occasionally turning the leaf to tap its reverse side. Display your leaf skeleton by gluing it to some coloured card then covering it in cellophane.

Find out what's happening in space

Check out this NASA pic of the day:

www://antwrp.gsfc.gov/apod/

Look – no hands! Make a pooter

23

Think how many thousands of times bigger you are than an ant or woodlouse. Then imagine you're being picked up by a monstrous great creature thousands of times bigger than *you* are! And think of the damage it might do to you, even if it doesn't mean to.

Sometimes, when we try to pick up a fast-moving tiny creature, no matter how careful or gentle we are, we can seriously hurt it, or at least cause it pain. A pooter is a really useful little gizmo that allows you to pick up mini-critters without touching or hurting them.

WHAT YOU NEED:

- A small jar with a plastic lid
- A drill
- Two lengths of plastic tubing – 20 cm (8 in) and 30 cm (12 in)
- Your tame adult

Here's how to make one.

WHAT TO DO:

- Ask your tame adult to drill two holes in the plastic lid for you.
- Push the lengths of tube through the holes so that they are halfway down the inside of the jar.
- Now find an insect and, having placed the end of the longer tube over it, give a careful suck on the end of the short tube. The vacuum you create in the tubes will now cause the insect to be sucked up into the jar.

WARNING:

Don't suck too hard or you may end up with a mouthful of earwig!

Learn how to conjure up stunning mini-beast snaps with your pocket digital camera

Most digital cameras will allow you to take a photo from as close as 10 cm and some will allow you to get even closer.

TOP TIPS FOR MARVELLOUS MINI-BEAST PHOTOS:

- If you're less than a metre from your critter, switch off the built-in flash.

- If your camera has a close-up or 'macro' mode it can be set to allow you to get even closer to your subject, even as close as 2 cm!

- Most pocket cameras have a zoom lens. Zoom in on your critter to really 'big-up' the image!

- If it has it, make sure your camera's image stabilisation is switched on. It makes up for any shakiness, giving you sharper pictures in low light.

TOP TIP!

Don't forget! If you see some really amazing wildlife action and don't have your camera to hand you can always capture the moment on your mobile phone camera. It may even have a video facility.

Sleep tight and hope the bugs DO bite!
Make a 'pitfall trap'

Lots of creepy crawlies are nocturnal. In other words, they wander around our gardens, parks, woods and fields in the dead of night (along with all the usual vampires, zombies and werewolves). Here's a way to trap and examine these fascinating creatures without having to stay up all night.

WHAT YOU NEED:
- A piece of wood or slate
- A trowel
- A small bowl
- A saucer
- A glass jar
- Four large stones and some 'bait', such as biscuit crumbs, bits of fruit or cheese (or fresh blood, if you're intending to trap a vampire)

See mini-beasts on the big screen!

Your microscope may well be linkable to your computer with a USB lead. So rather than peering into the eyepiece you can check out the action on your computer screen and share it with your friends and family.

WHAT TO DO:

- Dig a hole in the ground large enough to hold your glass jar.
- Put the jar in it and pack the soil around it tightly so the jar's rim is level with the surface. Put your bait in the jar.
- Place four small stones on the soil around the jar's rim and put the piece of wood or slate on top of them so that rain doesn't get in and drown your captives. Go to bed, sleep tight (and hope the bugs *do* bite!).

In the morning you can take the lid off your pitfall trap and check out your catch by emptying them into the bowl. Make a note of what you've caught and do drawings or take photographs of them. Release your captives into the wild (with a stern warning never to misbehave again!). Now reset your trap with different bait to see if it attracts different sorts of 'night creepers'.

Check out tree town!

Many trees are home to thousands and thousands of living things. For example, at least 450 different sorts of creatures live in an oak tree, including oak-bark beetles, nut weevils, gall wasps, gypsy moths, squirrels and dozens of different kinds of birds including owls, woodpeckers, treecreepers and nuthatches.

FASCINATING FACT!

Mull over a meadow brown. These lovely brown and orange butterfly have black eye spots on their forewings and their caterpillars feed on grass. So, guess why they're called meadow browns?

Simple pond dipping (for simple pond-dippers)

This is the sort of pond dipping which was carried out in ye olden days by children who were born before the invention of newfangled contraptions such as iPods and warm trousers. You can do this by tightly tying a length of string around the neck of a jam jar (or, if you're posh, a sun-dried tomato jar). 'Brace' the string by tying another length under the bottom of the jar and make sure you've got enough string to be able to sling your jar a good way if you wish.

The jar should be empty before you dip, however, you may wish to 'bait' your jar with a few damp breadcrumbs in order to attract little fish. Now lower your jar into the water at the edge of the pond, wait a while, then carefully and slowly lift your jar out of the water. If you're lucky you may well be delighted to discover that your jar is now teeming with all manner of wriggly, twitchy little creatures including water fleas, tadpoles, great diving beetles, water snails, pondskaters (and tiny alligators). But if it isn't, don't despair, simply dip again.

Daring pond dipping

For adventurous pond-dippers, show-offs, eco-warriors and sophisticated types.

WHAT YOU NEED:

- A net (The ones sold in seaside shops are OK, but they are a bit flimsy. You can get better nets from fish-keeping suppliers. However, make sure the holes are small enough to catch the little squigglers, but not so small that they will pick up half a tonne of mud when you scoop.)
- Containers, filled with a little water, to keep your captives in – plastic ice-cream tubs are good for this (though why you're eating plastic ice-cream is anyone's guess). You can also buy small transparent 'observation' pots. They even have lids which double as a magnifying glass.
- Spoons (for transferring small animals between containers).
- A magnifying glass, for looking at tiny pond life.

WHAT TO DO:

Try to develop a technique in which you use your net to 'sweep' a figure-of-eight pattern in the water for about ten seconds. Whilst you're 'sweeping', try to avoid scooping up the muddy gloop from the bottom of the pond and the pondweed from the top, or you'll find it really hard to see what you've caught. Now smoothly raise your net from the water, carry it to your containers, then making sure it's actually in the water, turn it inside out, swish it about a bit and release all the little miracles you've just 'bagged'.

Study tiny creatures using a microscope

If you've never peered at an ant, freshwater shrimp or a greenfly through a microscope, you've missed out on a whole lot of fun. And you're also in for a BIG shock. Because once you're 'face-to-face' with your subject, you won't even recognise it as the tiny speck you just put under the lens!

You'll see that it has all sorts of fascinating details and features you could never have even guessed at when you were studying it with your naked eye!

Most experts would warn you against buying a 'toy' microscope, as the results are usually disappointing and may even put you off microscopy for ever. If you don't have a microscope, you may have one at school or at your local natural history society.

Dead bug. Scan do!

As well as photographing insects you can make pictures of them using your computer and scanner. Here's how to do it.

1. First choose your insect. Almost any sort will do, but the main thing is that it should be dead. And in 'dead good' condition i.e. with all its bits and pieces present and not all rotten, manky or chewed.

2. Once you have chosen the deceased insect for the starring role (let's call him Sid), carefully place him on your scanner screen. Do NOT close your scanner lid as this will reduce the insect to mush!

3. Now cover Sid and the scanner screen with a large piece of plain white paper or a plain white box. This will recreate the plain white inside of your scanner lid. If you use a box, it should be about 5 cm (2 in) high.

4. Set the resolution on your scanner. For insects that are 3 mm (0.25 in) or more long, set it to between 200 and 400 DPI (dots per inch). Smaller insects will need a resolution of 400 to 800 DPI.

5. Now press the scan button so that Sid's image is transferred to your computer.

6. You may now wish to move Sid around in order to get a variety of interesting shots, such as underneath or profile (pouting, cheeky, etc.)

Wild Things To Do With Grasshoppers

Imitate a grasshopper

You can imitate a male grasshopper's chirps simply by stroking a comb against the edge of a piece of cardboard. But beware! If you do this in a field at the height of summer you may be inundated with hundreds of lonely lady grasshoppers!

Catch a grasshopper

First, find your grasshopper. The best places are grassy fields and patches of weeds on sunny summer days.

If it's a male, your grasshopper will very sportingly guide you to the exact spot where it's hiding by rubbing a set of pegs on its back legs against its forewings, to make that familiar chirping sound. Actually, it's not your attention it's trying to attract, but that of female grasshoppers, who don't have nearly as much to say for themselves.

Once you've located your grasshopper, sneak up on it using some of the stealth skills you learned in pages 10-11.

Now put your hands together, as if you are going to say a prayer e.g. 'Please help me catch this grasshopper'. Now unfold your hands like a book, keeping your thumbs together.

Now cup your hands around the grasshopper as quickly as you can. Once it's inside the 'cup', transfer your grasshopper to your collecting jar. You can now examine it.

Keep some pet grasshoppers

It's best to keep the young grasshoppers, known as nymphs, as pets (they're far more playful and much easier to house-train). Grasshoppers don't do the egg/caterpillar/pupa/adult bit like so many other insects. They simply hatch from eggs as miniature versions of their adult selves. They then go through a series of moults where they shed their skin, getting bigger (and smarter) each time.

Keep your pet grasshoppers in a plastic aquarium with some net mesh on top to stop them from hopping out. Provide them with 'sunshine' by putting a lamp next to them during daylight hours. Remember to keep them out of direct sunlight or they'll just get frazzled.

Put a few twigs in to give them something to dangle from when they moult and feed them on a mixture of grasses. (Check out page 163 to find out about this.)

You'll need to change the grass regularly to keep it fresh and make sure your grasshoppers remain healthy. (Taking a sick grasshopper to the vet is a nightmare and the bills can be horrendous!)

IMPORTANT:

Don't keep your grasshoppers indefinitely. When you've seen a few of the spectacular striptease shows which are their moults, release them in the place you found them.

Wild Things To Do With Woodlice

Make a woodlouse maze out of Lego

Once you've designed your Lego maze, cover the bricks in clingfilm to stop the little rascals from climbing out. Now, let them loose! You should find that the woodlice invariably turn left at the first T junction they get to (unless it happens to have a No Entry sign).

35 Keep some woodlice as pets

Woodlice make great pets. They can be found under stones, rotten tree bark, plant pots (and teachers' armpits). And they're absolutely free! What's more, you hardly ever have to take them to the vet (well, not unless they happen to break a leg or catch a cold). To keep woodlice, you'll need a margarine tub with some damp soil in it and some kitchen waste – preferably the vegetable sort, as they aren't all that keen on eating empty yoghurt pots and marmite jars.

Don't worry if you forget to feed your woodlice every once in a while. They are quite happy to sort out their own tea by eating their own poo (filthy beasts!)

Oh look! Lunch

Count a woodlouse's legs

This is trickier than you might think! Woodlice spend most of the time waggling their legs around quite infuriatingly. So, simply pop a few woodlice in the fridge for a minute or so to 'chill-out'. This will have the effect of calming them down so that they stay still long enough for you to do the leg census. However, don't leave them in there for too long or they'll become 'woodl-*ice*'.

Identify the make and model of your woodlice

Out of the staggering (scurrying and scampering) 3,500 different types of woodlice in the world, there are about 35 different sorts here in the United Kingdom.

Take macro woodlice snaps

Use the macro facility on your digital camera to take some cheesy family snaps of your woodlice at work, rest and play.

On the web

Learn how to care for your woodlice. Check out the YouTube video which shows you how to do just that!

http://www.youtube.com/watch?v=k8hlZppM7cc

Wild Things To Do With Woodlice

41 Find a bagful of babies

Gently flip a few of your woodlice onto their backs and check them out with your magnifying glass. You'll eventually discover one with a white or yellow pouch between its front legs. This will be a female woodlice and the pouch will either contain a clutch of woodlouse eggs or a brood of baby woodlice who are biding their time before they launch themselves into the extremely scary big wide world of hungry frogs, hedgehogs, blackbirds (and junior naturalists).

42 Observe your woodlice through a large magnifying glass

Amongst the amusing tricks they get up to, you will see them drinking through their bottoms, eating their own poo, moulting and looking after their children. (And juggling spiders!)

Something not to do with your woodlice

The mother of Isaac Asimov, the science-fiction author, became alarmed when she noticed that her young son (before he became a well-known author) had a very strange expression on his face. When she asked him what the problem was he didn't say a word, so she became even more alarmed, believing him to have been struck dumb. However, a moment later all was revealed; Isaac opened his mouth to reveal that he'd stuffed it full of live woodlice. Apparently he'd put them in there to 'see if they'd tickle' when they walked about on his tongue.

43 Guess which one of these names for woodlice is made-up

Here are some of the daft names dreamed up for woodlice by olden-days people who had nothing better to do with their time: Bibble Bugs, Cheesy Bugs, Cud-Worms Coffin-Cutters, Roly Polys, Monkey Peas, Penny Pigs, Sink-Lice, Slaters, Sowbugs, Tinkling Rachels, and Tiggyhogs.

Answer: Tinkling Rachels

44 Say 'cheerio' to your woodlice

And finally, if you become bored with your woodlice, don't cruelly dump them in the fast lane of the M1, just release them into the wild again! Remember: a woodlouse is for life – not just for Christmas!

Measure the height of a tree without climbing it

Some trees have been around yonks and are mega-massive. For instance, the 'Ankerwyke' yew tree at Runnymede in Berkshire is 9.4 metres (31 feet) wide and an astonishing *2,000* years old! It's been around so long that it's said to have witnessed the signing of the Magna Carta by King John in 1215 (but, being a tree, it couldn't make head nor tail of it). If you want to find out the height of a really big tree you'll need a long measuring stick and a friend to help you. First measure your friend's height and make a note of it. Now get your friend to stand at the tree's base.

Date a tree

Take a tape measure and wrap it around the tree trunk at about 1 metre (3 feet) above the ground. Now divide that measurement by 2.5 and the answer will be the age of the tree. The 'waists' of adult trees grow by about 2.5 centimetres every year (just like the waists of grown-ups).

Move a good distance away from the tree, telling your friend to stand perfectly still until you tell them they can move.

Next, hold a stick at arm's length and line up the top of the stick with the top of your friend's head. Now mark the stick where it lines up with your friend's feet. Remaining in exactly the same position, see how many times you can fit the marked section of the stick into the height of the tree. Multiply that number by your friend's height and you'll get the approximate height of the tree (and a sore arm).

Find out how old a cut-down tree is

If you look at the cut section of the tree's trunk you'll see a series of rings, one inside the other. These are the tree's annual growth rings. It adds one every year. Yes, we get birthdays; trees get rings! By counting the rings you can work out the age of the tree.

WARNING!

Do not deliberately cut down a tree to age it. Trees take years to grow and are absolutely vital to the well-being of our environment (and more to the point, the wood sprites will get you if you do!)

Distinguish springwood from summerwood

Look carefully at the tree's growth rings and you'll see that they have a light section and a dark section. The light section is called the springwood. It's usually the widest because a tree does most of its growing in the spring. The narrowest, dark section is called the summerwood because the tree's growth rate slows down in the summer before stopping completely in the autumn and winter.

Carry out a survey of 16 cm² (6 in²) of soil

Huge areas of our planet are seething with all manner of mini-beasts. But we don't see them because they're very small, very shy, under the ground (or on their holidays). In this activity you can discover what a rich and diverse selection of squigglers, squirmers and wrigglers inhabit a very small area of ground.

Find some soil. It could be a little-used corner of your garden, the leafy floor of a forest, or the boggy edge of a pond. Mark out a square measuring 16 cm on each side. For this you could use a gadget known as a quadrat, which is simply four pieces of wood or plastic tubing fixed together. Place it over the spot you wish to survey and mark the boundaries.

When you've marked out your hunting ground, begin to carefully remove the top few centimetres of soil using a small garden trowel. Now gently sift through the soil with your fingers, making a note of all the little animals you find. Use your pooter (see page 16) or a white plastic spoon to examine them in more detail. Keep a record of the depth at which you found the creatures, how many there were and what exactly they looked like. Now dig up a few more centimetres of soil and see if the creatures deeper down differ from those nearer the surface.

Remember to carefully replace the creatures and the soil when you've finished.

Bean there, grown that!

Seeds are astonishing. Programmed into them is not only a future plant, but all the instructions for what that plant will be like, including its structure, its taste, its texture and its colour! Which means that if you plant a carrot seed, it will grow into a carrot, rather than a potato or a cauliflower (or a hamster). And if you plant a broad bean seed it will grow into a broad bean, as we will now discover!

WHAT TO DO:

WHAT YOU NEED:

- A broad bean
- A cow to exchange for the bean (if you don't happen to have any money)
- A tall glass
- Some cotton wool
- A sheet of blotting paper
- Scissors

Line the inside of your glass with the blotting paper then stuff it full of cotton wool. Squidge your broad bean between the blotting paper and the glass. Half fill the glass with water. Watch carefully over the next few days, remembering to keep the cotton wool moist! You should be able to see the miracle of life and growth taking place as the broad bean seed thrusts out roots and forces its stem skywards. Rejoice!

NB: If your bean plant does happen to grow extra, extra tall, perhaps reaching a giant's castle in the clouds where you discover a goose which lays golden eggs and makes you extremely rich, please remember who told you how to grow the bean in the first place.

JACK
& the
BEANSTALK

Wild Things To Do With Ponds

Choose a position for your pond

This is a big and exciting project but it does involve a bit of careful planning, patience and hard work. You will also need your tame adult to help with this one. But rest assured, it will be well worth it in the end! And, unlike your bit of 'outdoors / indoors' freshwater aquarium, your pond will not just be home to aquatic creatures such as great diving beetles, daphnia and water fleas but it will also attract all sorts of other wildlife including swallows, frogs, toads, dragonflies, herons (herds of thirsty zebras, wildebeest and giraffes).

Choose a level area of your garden that gets plenty of shade. (Avoid overhanging trees and wet hollows, as you don't want your pond full of leaves in the Autumn and you don't want it flooding in wet weather. Mark out the shape of your pond using canes and string. Your pond will look more 'natural' and interesting if it is an irregular shape).

Make it as big as you possibly can. This will increase the variety of habitats available to the different wildlife that will be attracted to your pond. The edges should be shallow (so creatures can walk in and out quite easily, rather than having to dive in or perform embarrassing bellyflops and plants can rest on the edges). It also means that if the odd dimwitted hedgehog falls in it will be able to get out without too much trouble.

Make the middle of your pond at least 100 cm (40 in) deep so that the animals have somewhere to go when the rest of it freezes over in the winter.

Line your pond

Rake the surface of the pond bottom so that it's nice and smooth, and pick out all the sharp stones that might puncture your pond liner. Now cushion the bottom of your pond with sand or you could buy a professional underlay. Make sure you cushion the pond edges, too, as they are most likely to be punctured by sharp objects.

The best liners are made from stuff called butyl, which will last for at least twenty years. Make sure you buy more than the actual area of the pond, so that you can leave a generous overlap around the edge. Stretch your liner over the hole and gently smooth it into place.

Temporarily weigh down the edges using heavy but smooth objects such as bricks or big stones. Now cover the edges of the liner with soil or (round) gravel to a depth of about 10 cm.

Wild Things To Do With Ponds

Bit cramped isn't it?

Fill your pond

The best thing to fill your pond with is tap water and a hosepipe.

If you do use tap water, leave it in the pond for at least a week before introducing any wildlife, as this will allow the chlorine to evaporate. You can add a few buckets of rainwater if you wish, to help 'naturalise' the pond water.

Keep filling your pond until it's full to the brim. Smooth the liner down around the edge of the pond and trim the big floppy bits off so that you are left with a neat 30 cm (12 in) overlap.

Now dig a narrow trench all the way around the pond edge and tuck your overlapping liner into it before refilling it with soil so that it's completely hidden.

Remember, this is a 'natural' pond so the last thing you want to see is an unsightly black pond liner poking out.

Look after your wildlife pond

In the autumn, clear away the fallen leaves from your pond's surface so you don't get too many sinking to the bottom and rotting. Also remove some weeds, or it will become choked by the faster growing ones.

If your pond gets covered in blanket weed, pull it out by hand. A good way to remove duckweed is to scoop it out with a net.

IMPORTANT!

Leave the cleared weed on the edge of your pond for a few days, so that any creatures you've accidentally scooped out with it can crawl back into the water. You can then put the weed on the compost heap you made (see page 50).

In the depths of winter your pond may ice over completely, depriving its inhabitants of oxygen. Get a grown-up to hold a saucepan of hot water on the ice until it melts. You must not break the pond ice with a hammer. The shock waves will harm the little creatures living there.

ALSO IMPORTANT!

Don't put fish such as goldfish, shubunkins, orfe or Japanese koi (or piranhas, or sharks) in your pond, as they will eat the other inhabitants. If you do want to keep ornamental fish, it's best to make a separate pond for them.

Wild Things To Do With Ponds

Stock your wildlife pond

You can do this by simply leaving your pond alone. Word will soon spread amongst local dragonflies, frogs, beetles, toads, damselflies (and alligators) that there's a really cool new place to hang out and, after a while, you'll see all sorts of wildlife checking it out.

However, if you wish, you can add a few buckets of water collected on one of your pond dipping expeditions: this 'soup of life' will soon get the party started.

Important: Do not transfer buckets between ponds. It might spread disease.

Get to know a great water boatman

Great water boatmen are big beetles that swim upside-down just below the surface of the water using their hairy back legs as paddles. They can also fly really well (but are absolutely rubbish at the 100-metre sprint). They eat water fleas, small insects which have landed on the water surface, and mites by thrusting their 'beak' into them and sucking out their insides.

Listen to a lesser water boatman

If you've got lesser water boatmen in your freshwater pond listen out for the 'squeak' the males produce when they rub their front legs on the side of their head in order to attract mates.

Watch a water spider

Water spiders ingeniously devised a way of taking their air supply underwater with them long before the first scuba pioneers came up with the idea of oxygen tanks. These cunning little arachnids use the fine hairs on their abdomens to carry tiny bubbles of air around with them when they're submerged. This makes them look sparkly all over!

If you're lucky enough to see a water spider at breeding time, you'll notice that the spider makes a bell-shaped nest out of silk which they then fill with air so that their new families have something to breathe. Some young water spiders live in empty snail shells, which are great for filling with air.

Peer at a pond snail

Pond snails eat algae, lay their eggs on pond plants, can grow 6 centimetres tall (and are absolutely delicious with garlic and mayonnaise). If you see one of your pond snails floating upside down on the surface of the water, don't worry, it's not sunbathing, and it's not dead. It's just taking air into its single, simple lung before it submerges again.

Can you see a whirligig beetle in your pond?

These oddly named creatures really do exist but you have to look carefully because they are really small. If you look carefully you can see masses of them whirling like crazy on the surface of ponds. Their eyes are divided so that the top half can see above the water and the bottom half below the water at the same time. It is thought that they all whirl together to confuse predators, such as frogs and birds.

Watch some mini-beasts doing what comes naturally

Generally speaking, nature is ferocious and unforgiving. Many creatures live in constant fear of being eaten by bigger and fiercer creatures. (Yes, just like school.) Consequently, they spend almost all of their time cowering in dark, hidden places. If you put a square of white cloth on the ground with some weeds in the middle, then collect some mini-beasts and put them on it, you should see them instantly scuttle for the safety of the weeds (unless they happen to be really stupid).

Photograph a rainbow

But you'll have to be quick! And you'll have to be even quicker if you want to dash across this multi-coloured bridge to the land of the gods. Which is what the Vikings believed it was!

Watch some ants milking greenfly

If you carefully observe a cluster of greenfly on a plant you may be fortunate enough to see them being 'milked' by ants. Some species of ants love the 'honeydew' that the greenfly produce from plant sap. Look carefully and you may see the ants gently stroking the greenfly with their antennae, in order to get the honeydew flowing (and with the aid of a really powerful microscope, you'll also be able to see their little buckets, churns and milking stools).

Enjoy a thunderstorm!

Best done on a Thor's day (*Thursday*). Well, he was the Viking god of thunder. When the Vikings heard the claps and rumbles of thunder, they believed it was Thor, up in the mountains going bananas with his big hammer.

On the web

Here's an internet link to a photograph of a ladybird 'snacking on' a greenfly.

www.flickr.com/photos/
photomack/3405573804/

Work out how far away a storm is

Count the seconds between the lightning and thunder and divide by five. It takes about five seconds for the sonic boom to travel one mile, so if you see a streak of lightning and count 20 seconds until you hear the low rumble of the thunder, the storm is about four miles away (or your TV has just exploded).

FASCINATING SPIDER FACTS!

There are an average of 50,000 spiders scuttling around every single acre of land in Britain. Which means you're never more than a metre away from a spider (or four metres away from someone with arachnophobia). Long tailed tits use spider webs to build their nests. The Goliath bird-eating spider of South America can be as big as a dinner plate and its prey includes lizards, bats, snakes and birds. Spitting spiders live in the dark corners of houses and zap mosquitoes and house-flies with a sort of toxic glue that they, yes, you guessed it ... spit!

Wild Things To Do With Ladybirds

67 Watch some ants defending greenfly from ladybirds

Ants love to snack on honeydew, or greenfly poo, as it's otherwise known (weirdos!). And ladybirds love to snack on greenfly. So if ants catch a ladybird munching one of their little 'honeydew cows' they launch a full-scale attack. If you don't get to see it for real check out these great photos of the battle action!

http://www.pbase.com/antjes/lady_bug

WHAT YOU NEED:
- Five or six ladybird larvae
- A clear plastic box
- Some damp kitchen paper
- Some leaves
- 10 billion greenfly

Hunt some ladybird larvae

Looking at ladybird larvae it's hard to believe that these ugly little creatures could turn into anything quite as lovely as ladybirds. Search plants such as stinging nettles and thistles in June and July and you'll find these grey six-legged beetles with their orange spots and bristley warts which are going to turn into drop dead gorgeous ladybirds, as you'll now discover …

Watch the Beast turn into Beauty

WHAT TO DO:

Put your larvae in the box with the leaves and kitchen paper and keep them well supplied with greenfly. **NB**: If they run out, the little monsters will just eat each other! When you're not watching them gobble greenfly, make sure you regularly clean out their enclosure. They'll moult a

Alarm a ladybird

As you scoop up the ladybird, you may be amazed/horrified/delighted to see it squirt some revolting-looking, pongy yellow liquid from its leg joints. This is what is known as 'reflex-bleeding', and it's the ladybird's way of defending itself from predators such as hedgehogs, birds (and you). Does it work? Of course it does! You didn't eat the ladybird, did you?

Watch some ladybirds munching greenfly

If you don't see greenfly being milked by ants, you may see them being eaten by ladybirds. Here's an internet link to a photograph of a ladybird 'offing' a greenfly.

http://www.flickr.com/photos/photomack/3405573804/

Liberate a ladybird

If you find a ladybird trapped indoors, carefully scoop it up with a bit of tissue paper and put it outside before it starves to death (or dies of boredom).

few times, then you'll see them go all sulky and turn into pupae. About two weeks later a very plain-looking ladybird will crawl from the case, hang around for a few days, then transform into a stunningly attractive insect.

Drama queen

Why, I'm so gorgeous!

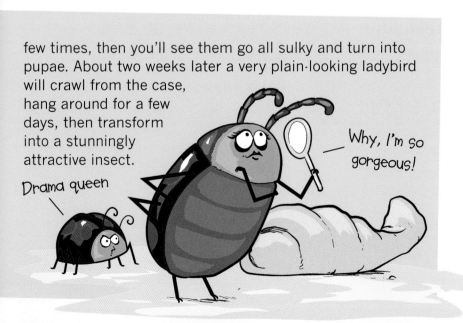

73 Learn to recognise three different sorts of clouds

- Cumulus: 'a cloud heap' – separate, piled-up, fluffy and different sizes
- Stratus: 'a cloud layer' – flat, unbroken sheets, often grey
- Cirrus: means a 'curl of hair' – these clouds are white and wispy
- Once you get to know these, learn three more. For instance: nimbus, altostratus and altocumulus.

75 Keep a cloud and weather record

Look at the clouds once or twice a day and make note of the date and time, the place, the kinds of clouds you see, the temperature and the weather.

74 Find out if it always rains more on Bank holidays by making your own rain gauge

WHAT YOU NEED:

- A clear plastic ruler
- A glass jar
- Two rubber bands
- A plastic funnel which will fit into the jar so that its rim is in line with its top edge
- Some rain!

WHAT TO DO:

Attach the ruler to the outside of the jar using the rubber bands. It's really important to make sure that the bottom edge of the ruler is in line with the bottom of the jar. Put your funnel in the jar.

Take your rain gauge outside (it always tends to rain more here), then place it somewhere well away from trees and buildings. Wait for it to rain.

76

Learn the colours of the rainbow with this easy reminder

Richard Of York Gave Battle In Vain = Red Orange Yellow Green Indigo Violet.

77

Make your own cloud

When warm, moist air rises into cold air that is high in the atmosphere, the water vapour condenses into larger water droplets which create clouds (and miserable holiday makers). To make your own cloud, put some ice in a small aluminium foil container like the ones you get takeaway in. Now put some warm water in the bottom of a tall vase or drinking glass. Put your ice container on top of the glass. Watch carefully! In a very short time your own little cloud will appear near the top of the glass.

When it's rained, read the ruler or sticky tape to find out how much rain has fallen and write down the measurements in your weather diary.

Empty your rain gauge after each measurement. Why not save the rainwater in a bucket and use it to top up the aquarium or tadpole tank you made in activities 118–122.

Wild Things To Do At Night

Check out the night sky

Binoculars and telescopes aren't just for watching wildlife. You can also use them to observe those other mysterious and magnificent miracles of nature up above us: the moon, the stars, the planets in our solar system and the Milky Way (plus the odd Mars bar, Curly Wurly or Galaxy). Of course, the time to do this is at night. And the best place to do it is where there aren't lots of streetlights or much light coming from windows. So, star-gazing somewhere well away from cities would be ideal. But if you can't manage this, don't worry; it's still possible. The main thing to remember when you're sky-watching is that your body is going to be in an awkward position and that you're going to be holding up your hands and arms for long periods of time. So get comfortable and stay as relaxed as you can. You can do this by lounging in a comfy chair as you survey the heavens, or leaning against a tree or wall, or even by just lying flat on your back. If you don't have binoculars, don't worry- you'll still see lots of exciting things!

Draw the moon

While you're checking it out through your 'bins', why not draw the moon? As you're sketching, you may well see the 'Man in the Moon', or 'The Hare' (or even Buzz Aldrin).

I've caught your dark side

Moon watch!

It's best to look at the moon through your binoculars or telescope when it's not full. In other words, when only part of it is illuminated by the sun's rays. When the moon's full there are no shadows on its surface so it's hard to make out any detail. However, if it's in a quarter stage you'll be able to see its craters because they'll be casting shadows. The longest shadows occur when the moon is close becoming a new moon so that's when its surface will be at its most interesting (and most *cheesy*).

Wild Things To Do At Night

Do some star gazing

Try looking even further into space using a small telescope and you'll even be able to see the planet Jupiter, its moons and Saturn and its rings. By looking through either a telescope or binoculars you should also get a good eyeful of the Milky Way itself. The Milky Way is the spiral-shaped galaxy that we live in which is made up of about 100-thousand-million stars all revolving around its centre.

All of these thousands of millions of stars are suns and, just like our sun, they have their own planets revolving around them. It's estimated that there are at least 200 billion of them. And, no doubt, on a few of those planets there is some sort of life going on (perhaps schools with see-through children and three-headed teachers?) What's more, beyond the Milky Way there are at least another 200 *billion* galaxies! And that's just in the part of the Universe that astronomers are able to observe. Makes your head whirl, doesn't it?

You might feel like going for a lie down after trying to get to grips with that sort of information. But then again, perhaps you *are* already lying down!

Camp out at night and record nocturnal sounds

The safest place to do this is in your own garden. If you do it anywhere else, such as the local woods, make sure you're accompanied by an adult and have permission to be there. With luck, you'll hear all sorts of exciting noises, including hooting owls, barking foxes, croaking frogs and snuffling hedgehogs (and howling banshees and snarling moths). Use the recording tips you read about in activity 215.

Make a grapefruit trap (for nocturnal mini-beasts)

This is an easy way to discover what sort of nocturnal mini-beasts are rampaging around your garden and partying on your patio while you're off in the Land of Nod.

WHAT TO DO:

Get your grown-up to cut the grapefruit in half. Scoop out the flesh with the spoon. Eat it (the flesh, not the spoon). In the evening, place the two halves of the grapefruit face-down in different parts of your garden. The next morning, turn over the skins to discover what night-creepers

WHAT YOU NEED:

• A grapefruit
• A spoon
• A knife
• A chopping board
• Your tame grown-up

have been lured into your traps. There should be at least a few snails, slugs, woodlice and beetles in there. If your traps do happen to be empty it might suggest that someone has been going crazy with all those nasty, environmentally unfriendly pesticides which do so much damage to our native wildlife. Perhaps it's time to have a quiet word about saving the planet?

Make a compost heap

One of the biggest problems with our planet is that people are constantly taking things from the environment and never putting much back in its place, apart from pollutants! But it doesn't have to be like that. Lots of people throw away things which are really, really valuable! Not diamond rings or gold bars. They chuck away things like potato peelings, coffee grounds, tea bags, cabbage leaves and banana skins! And what happens to these little treasures? They're bunged in dirty great pits known as landfill sites.

Not only is this harming our environment, but it's also a terrible waste. Because, with time and effort, all those potato peelings, bits of orange peel and apple cores can be recycled and turned into the sweet smelling, rich, dark, crumbly, life-giving stuff known as compost. At least 40% of the stuff that some people put in dustbins is suitable for recycling. Why not do your bit towards improving the

Be a little Tommy rotter

The air around us is absolutely heaving with millions of different sorts of bacteria. And some of them are very, very destructive. Watch them devastate a date or pulverise a pepper!

For this example, we'll use little Tommy tomato as our victim. First ask your tame grown-up to slice him in two. Now put his two halves on a plate and leave him alone in a warm place. During the next few weeks, moulds and bacteria will wreak havoc with the poor little chap, changing his shape, colour and texture, eventually reducing him to a little heap of pathetic mush! Create a fascinating but gruesome record of his descent into disgusting detritus by photographing him each day.

environment by making a compost heap. There are several ways you can do this. You can buy ready-made compost bins or make DIY ones from old wooden pallets, or concrete blocks, or one of those huge bags that builders' merchants deliver sand and gravel in.

Get to know this checklist of some of the things you CAN and CAN'T recycle on your compost heap:

CAN:

Nettles; grass clippings; raw vegetable peelings; tea bags and tea leaves; coffee grounds; fallen leaves; wood ash; hair; nail clippings; crushed egg shells; hay, straw or shredded paper bedding from herbivorous pets such as rabbits and guinea pigs.

CAN'T:

Meat; fish; cooked food; coal ash; cat litter; dog dirt; disposable nappies.

Spread the bad news about slug pellets

The slug is the number one enemy of gardening grown-ups. In a single night a posse of rampaging slugs can devastate a bed of flowers or vegetables that a hard-working gardener has nurtured with hours of tender loving care. So what do many grown-ups do? They rush out and buy the nasty things known as slug pellets. Not to shoot the slugs with but to poison them. In doing this they're not only killing slugs but they're also murdering innocent creatures which so helpfully snack on slugs. Tell the grown-ups that instead of using slug pellets they can protect their plants with barriers of fine grit, seaweed, pine needles or copper which the slugs don't like crawling over. When slugs touch copper, a reaction occurs between the copper and the slime giving them an electric shock They can also add nematodes to their soil. These microscopic worms get inside slugs then release bacteria which is fatal to them.

Wild Things To Do With Bird Food

Make a five-star bird restaurant

When it's absolutely freezing cold on a winter's night, *you* can turn up the heating, put on an extra fleece and snuggle up in bed. But wild birds can't! They have to endure snow, rain, gales and sub-zero temperatures without so much as a woolly hat or a pair of thermal undies. One way you can help birds to survive sub-zero temperatures is to make them a huge, steaming bowl of bird pudding. (And don't worry, it doesn't contain a single bird!) It's packed with energy-giving ingredients that their little bodies will convert to heat.

INGREDIENTS:

Peanuts, sunflower seeds and other assorted bird seeds, kitchen scraps such as hard cheese or bacon rind, sultanas, raisins, chopped figs, plain flour and lard or suet.

WHAT TO DO:

Soften the suet or lard by kneeding it in your hands. The warmth of your hands will make it soft enough to squish all the other ingredients into it. Once everything's joined together in a big, sticky blob... your gourmet bird-pudding is ready!

WARNING:

If you have a nut allergy, avoid adding the peanuts and make sure the seed mixture doesn't contain nuts.

Make your five-star bird restaurant safe

Place all of your bird food well away from bushes and other hiding places, so that the feasting feather-brains have a good all-round view and aren't surprised by marauding cats and hawks.

Hang up a dangling bird feeder

Fill this with striped sunflower or niger seeds for greenfinches, siskins, goldfinches and tits. These birds all prefer to feed high up from the ground.

Hang up some coconuts

Fill half an empty coconut shell with bird pudding and hang from tree branches.

Put out a treat for long-tailed tits

Smear bird pudding on tree trunks. The sociable little long-tailed tits are able to grip the bark with their strong claws and hang onto the tree trunks as they peck at the pudding.

Tweet your bird feeders to a spring clean

Clean your bird feeders regularly to prevent disease.

I've had nothing to eat all day

Wild Things To Do With Bird Food

Send nature nuts!

Put some peanuts in a wire-mesh bird feeder and if you're lucky you might see coal tits, blue tits, great tits, great spotted woodpeckers, nuthatches and siskins pecking away at these high-energy treats. Make sure you clean out the nuts that have gone black and squidgy in the bottom of the feeder. And DON'T use salted or dry-roasted peanuts in your feeder!

Set up a bird table

A bird table is an excellent way of protecting birds from prowling pussycats. You can put all sorts of food on your bird table including mixed seeds, bits of suet, bacon scraps and bird pudding. Make sure your bird table has a rim to prevent scraps falling off it, clean it regularly and remove mouldy uneaten food.

Save a chick from choking

During bird breeding season, make sure no whole peanuts are left lying around. Parent birds may feed them to their chicks, causing them to choke.

And this is where our mealworm army will attack the humans

Make a mealworm sandwich!

Mealworms are brilliant nosh for birds, but they're really expensive. Breed your own by following these simple instructions. Your birds will love you for it!

WHAT TO DO:

Punch small holes in the lid of a biscuit tin, put a layer of sacking in the bottom and sprinkle it with bran. Then add a slice or two of bread and raw potato on top. Now repeat this until you've got a 'three-decker' sandwich. Now top it off with a raw cabbage leaf and add 200 mealworms. Keep your tin at room temperature and, after a few weeks, the mealworms will turn into cream-coloured pupae, then into absolutely adorable little beetles. The beetles will lay eggs, which will hatch into yet more mealworms, which will then turn into more pupae, then more beetles. (Before you know it, the evil little blighters will be hatching a plan for world domination.) Now feed a bunch of them to your birds.

WARNING:

Never eat your mealworms, even if they do look tasty!

Tame a robin with some live mealworms

If you put out mealworms for a robin, gradually placing them nearer and nearer to where you're standing, you may find that you'll eventually be able to get the robin to land on your hand. You'll need to be patient though. Taming a robin can take weeks.

Lure some bats with mealworms

It's not just birds that like mealworms. See if you can get swooping bats to snatch mealworms in mid-flight by catapulting them into the air while they're hunting.

Sprinkle some pastry 'maggots'

This tasty recipe for birds involves three parts flour and one part margerine. Just crumble them together with your fingers and sprinkle on the ground for the birds to enjoy.

Wild Things To Do With Bird Food

WHAT YOU NEED:
- A small log, about 40 cm (16 in) long
- A drill
- A tame grown-up to do the drilling
- String
- A screw eye
- Some bird 'pudding'

Make a triple-decker for a hungry woodpecker

One of the most spectacular and beautiful birds to visit our gardens is the great spotted woodpecker. Their striking black-and-white colouring, with its vivid dashes of blood red, really is an awe-inspiring sight. One you've seen your first great spotted woodpecker, you'll never forget it!

WHAT TO DO:

Drill 3 holes through the log. They should be about the width of a 10p piece and spaced about 10 cm (4 in) apart. Screw the screw-eye into the top of the log and attach a loop of string to it. Stuff the holes with bird-pudding.

When the woodpeckers discover your pudding log, they'll be delighted, hanging on to it and pecking away for all they're worth.

Where's this triple-decker?

Keep a summer garden diary

List and photograph all the things that visit your garden one summer.

_____

_____

_____

_____

_____

_____

_____

_____

_____

_____

_____

Stick your photos here

Wild Things To Do At The Beach

Don't ask

Go beachcombing

102

The tide comes in twice a day and, every time it does, it leaves a fresh hoard of treasure. All you have to do to beachcomb is walk along the strandline to discover some real surprises. All sorts of things have been found by beachcombers, including shells, starfish, dead swordfish, animal skeletons, jellyfish, shark egg cases, dead seahorses and messages in bottles.

WHAT TO DO:

Winter is probably the best time to go beachcombing, as that's when storms and high tides stir objects up from the depths of the ocean and sweep them ashore. However, each season has its own sort of treasures.

You must walk slowly and be patient. Use those 'eagle-eyes' to search for the odd-looking piles of sand and knots of seaweed which may be concealing something absolutely amazing.

Some beaches are better than others for beachcombing. There's a link listing some good ones at the end of this book.

WARNING!

While you're on the beach, take care! Don't ever turn your back on the tide or you may be caught out by an unexpectedly large and powerful wave which could sweep you out to sea. Also, be very careful about what you pick up. Some objects are sharp or dangerous. Watch out for the tar and oil which coats some objects – it's very hard to remove from your hands and clothes. And if you find a jellyfish, it's probably best to just look at it. It might still be alive, and be quite keen to sting you!

Make a seashell collection

While you're beachcombing, you'll find hundreds of beautiful seashells of different sorts. And every single one of those shells has been home to some sort of animal. Part of the fun of collecting seashells is discovering and learning the names of the creatures that once lived inside them. Creatures with names like slipper limpets, Portugese oysters, periwinkles, cockles and piddocks.

Most of these creatures belong to a group of animals called molluscs. Molluscs don't have a backbone and their shells are both their skeletons and their houses. You're likely to find the most shells on quieter beaches with less people around. Go shell collecting when the tide is out, because this gives you a bigger area to search for shells. Have a dig, too, because some shells are buried beneath the sand.

Collecting empty seashells means that you're not depriving an animal of its home, as their occupants are long gone. When you get your shells home, clean them with warm water, then set about identifying them. Once you've done this you can arrange them and show them off, perhaps with their name label next to them. You might like to 'shell out' for some special display drawers, like the ones you see in museums. Now you can tell everyone you're a conchologist, someone who studies seashells.

IMPORTANT NOTE!

It's much better to find shells for your collection on the beach. Shells in seaside shops are often from non-sustainable sources, so buying them is not good for the environment.

What other things could you collect whilst you're there?

What do you mean, collect?

Wild Things To Do At The Beach

Winkle out some winkles!

If you go to certain beaches you'll see flocks of wading birds including oystercatchers, sandpipers, curlews, greenshanks and turnstones feeding on the shoreline. It's really hard to see what they're eating, so why not find out by becoming a wading bird yourself and sifting hungrily through the sand and mud.

WHAT TO DO:

Start by digging to the same depth the wading birds do, then swirl your strainer full of sand in shallow water to discover your 'catch'.

Look for clues that indicate animals are lurking just beneath the surface! Study the wet sand and mud close to the low-tide mark and also look through the shallow water at the sand below. In the wet sand you'll see the 'casts' which squirt out of the rear ends of lugworms. There'll also be a little hollow in the sand where the lugworm's head is eating the sand. If you dig up a lugworm, which is the favourite nosh of curlews and godwits, you'll see that it looks like an earthworm that needs a shave.

You'll also unearth molluscs, such as cockles and tellin, which oystercatchers dig out with their long red beaks. Explore the sand in the shallow water and you'll find shrimps and the other little crustaceans that plovers catch with their short beaks.

105

Make a rock pool mirror viewer

Explore the 'secret' areas of rock pools by attaching a small mirror to strong bendy wire using extra sticky 'duct' tape.

106

Date a mollusc

Molluscs, such as cockles and whelks, leave growth lines on their shells, just like trees make annual growth rings inside their trunks. And it's even easier to see them on shellfish because the lines are on the outside. There's one line for each year the mollusc's been around!

What?
I just got up

I'm 86 you know?

107

Watch wet wildlife through polarized sunglasses

Put on a pair of polarized sunglasses and, peer into a pond, lake or river - and all will become CLEAR!

Wild Things To Do At The Beach

Learn to snorkel and get a fish's-eye view of the depths

108

You'll be astonished by your magical new underwater environment, complete with its hills and valleys, 'forests' of waving weeds, darting shoals of fish and other mysterious creatures. Addiction guaranteed!

Turn 'mermaids' tears' into jewellery

109

When you're beachcombing you'll find sea glass or 'mermaid's tears', as it's sometimes known. These are bits of glass that have been tumbled smooth by the waves and sand. Much of it is quite beautiful and, with the addition of a few jewellery-making extras, you can turn it into things like charm bracelets, rings and necklaces.

Claws!

110

Crabs are hungry, feisty crustaceans. But with their ten legs, two of which have morphed into fearsome claws, they're good fun to go fishing for.

To fish for crabs, all you need is a long piece of string with a chicken wing or some uncooked bacon rind tied on the end. You can fish from all sorts of spots including rocks, jetties, quaysides, bridges and beaches.

After a while, pull in your bait to see what little, or large, ten-legged terror is hanging on to it. Then transfer your catch to a plastic bucket filled with water so you can check out those spooky 'otherworldly' eyes on stalks and their lethal claws.

Go seal watching

111

Seals are great to watch and are so inquisitive that they'll often bob up in the water next to your boat so that they can get a good look at you, too!

Sometimes you'll find that a crab has only got one claw because it's had the other ripped off in a fight with a rival. Don't get your fingers too close to those claws or they may nip you!

PLEASE!

Remember to be gentle with your catches, keep them in a shady spot and return them to the place where you caught them - crabs have feelings too you know! If you want to go in for competitive crabbing, why not enter the annual British Open Crabbing Championship at Walberswick in Suffolk: www.walberswick.ws/crabbing

112 Count a handful of sand grains

Next time you're on a beach (or lost in the desert) scoop up some sand and count every single grain. Now try and imagine how many grains there are in the whole world, and you'll still come nowhere near to the number of stars there are in our universe!

113 Visit a seabird colony

There are more of these in the British Isles than anywhere else in the world!

At the height of the breeding season they're home to chaotic masses of mating, feeding and fighting seabirds. Thousands of people travel to witness these spectacular scenes every year. Unmissable!

114 Sniff a seabird colony

In addition to the chaotic noise and movement of the colony the other thing that will strike you is the awful pong. Once sniffed, never forgotten!

Photograph, sketch and measure wild plants in May and June and see which are the fastest growing

You can hardly fail to notice that by the time the merry month of May comes around nature is partying like crazy. Birds are mating and singing their hearts out, butterflies are flitting from flower to flower, fish are spawning and trees are blossoming. And wild weeds seem to be growing at a mile a minute. It seems that one week your local track, bit of waste ground or hedgerow is almost bare, and the next you can hardly get past it for all the nettles, cow parsley and brambles which seem to have sprung up from nowhere.

Before   After

Find out just how fast they are growing by selecting a group of those plants and measuring and photographing them every few days between the last week of May and the first week of June. Keep a record of your findings in your nature notebook. Cow parsley, nettles and blackberry brambles might be good subjects to begin with. You'll be *amazed* by the rate at which they grow!

WARNING:
While doing your investigations, be sure to protect yourself from those nettles and brambles by wearing gloves, trousers and a long-sleeved top.

Pucker up with some parasites

Mistletoe is a partly parasitic plant that grows on the branches of trees such as apple, hawthorn, lime and poplar.

After a bird (usually a mistle thrush) has eaten the berries then excreted them onto a branch, their sticky coating ensures they stay in place, no matter what the weather. When spring comes, the mistletoe seed sprouts, takes nutrients from the tree and begins to grow into a plant. If you want to grow your own mistletoe, save a sprig at Christmas and keep it in a jar of water on a windowsill in a cold but frost-free place.

Then, in February, find the branch of a tree which is about 20 cm (8 in) in diameter and stick about twenty mistletoe berries to its underside using their naturally 'gluey' coating. The following spring the first leaves will appear on your plant, but it will be another three years before you see the fully formed mistletoe growing on your tree.

Put up a nest box camera

If you've got a really handy (or rich) grown-up, why not ask them to set up a nest box with a built in camera in your garden so that you can watch the daily drama take place as birds hatch and feed their little ones. Alternatively check out webcams at this link:

http://www.rspb.org.uk/webcams/

Wild Things To Do With Water Creatures

WHAT YOU NEED:

- An aquarium i.e. a glass-sided fish tank
- A place to put your aquarium
- Gravel (Soil or sand will not do!) Gravel is available from pet shops.
- A few crack-free stones (Sandstone or granite are good, but don't use limestone)
- Plants, from a 'wet-pet' shop or a friend's pond

118 Bring a bit of outdoors, indoors! Create a freshwater aquarium

This is a really exciting and fascinating project where you can put together a complete microhabitat. In the microhabitat you can watch the comings and goings of all the strange little creatures that normally live out their mysterious lives hidden in the mud and weeds of natural ponds.

WHAT TO DO:

1. Choose a position for your aquarium. Ideally, it'll be a spot where you can keep an eye on the little citizens of the 'wet-world'. Whatever you do, don't position it in direct sunlight – the water may overheat and some of your water critters will die! Sunlight will also increase the growth of algae, which in turn causes the water to go a murky green colour.

2. Make sure your aquarium is clean - if there is any dirt or dead algae on the glass, scrub it off with a 'sponge' made from some wet newspaper. Prepare the gravel by washing it under a running tap until the water flows clean.

3. Now decorate your aquarium. Spread the gravel over the bottom about 25 mm (1 in) deep. Make sure it slopes towards the front of the tank so that all the grot and rubbish, such as snail poo, uneaten food, and rotting leaves (and old car tyres and abandoned supermarket trolleys) collects at the front.

Now add the stones. It's a good idea to boil the stones and then scrub them to make sure they're really clean. Get a grown-up to help you with this. (Just tell them you're making stone soup!)

4. Add the plants. If you do get them from a friend's pond, give them a really good wash before you put them in your tank (the plants, not your friend). Don't take plants from natural ponds as they're already in short supply in the wild. Also, don't put duckweed in your aquarium. It spreads at about a mile a minute and will soon cover the surface of your aquarium and cut out the light for all the other plants. Take all the dead and rotting leaves off your plants then push their roots or stem bases into the gravel. Also check the plant leaves for little clusters of snail eggs (they look like jelly). If you have too many, your aquarium will be taken over by snails which will eat all the plants. Leave just a few eggs on the leaves (and make yourself a little omelette with the rest).

5. Now you can add the water. The best way to do this is by placing two or three sheets of newspaper in the tank. Fold them so they fit neatly but aren't too tight. This will allow you to pour in the water without disturbing the plants or gravel. You can fill your tank with tap water, but pond water would be best.

6. Leave your tank to settle for a week before adding any fish.

I love what you've done with the place

Wild Things To Do With Water Creatures

Never be tempted to drink from an aquarium

Look after your aquarium

To keep your microhabitat in tip-top condition, you should clean the grot from the bottom by 'siphoning'. To do this, you'll need a bucket and a length of tube.

1. Place the bucket on the floor below the aquarium. Lower one end of the siphon tube into the aquarium water near the piled-up grot. Put the other end in your mouth and give it a swift suck. As soon as you see the mucky water coming up the tube whip it out of your mouth and put it in the bucket. Air pressure and gravity will keep the water running through the tube.

2. Now move the end of the tube around the gravel 'vacuuming' up the muck until it's all gone. Do this gently, taking care not to disturb plants and animals.

WARNING!

Try not to swallow any water when you suck. It tastes really horrible and can make you ill. And, of course, avoid drinking any little creatures. **NB:** If you don't fancy doing the sucking bit, you can buy a siphon with a squeezy ball on the end.

Breed some daphnia

Daphnia are often referred to as water fleas but they aren't really insects at all. They're actually tiny office workers with laptops. No, that's not true either! They're really tiny crustaceans with hard outer shells, closely related to creatures like crabs, crayfish and lobsters.

All sorts of water creatures love to eat daphnia, so if you want to feed the tadpoles, newts, water mites, and fish that live in your freshwater aquarium or pond on something really nourishing, why not breed a whole bunch of these cute little crustaceans.

1. Leave some buckets of water outside in bright sunlight for a few days, until the tiny plants known as algae form in it and send it a grotty green colour.

2. Buy some daphnia from a 'wet-pet' shop and put them in one of the buckets. The little tinkers will now begin gobbling the algae and multiplying like crazy!

Well, not quite like that. The water will begin to go clear, as they gobble up the algae. That means it's time to feed some of the daphnia to your fish and tadpoles, whilst transferring the remainder to the next bucket of green water so that you can keep your stock going.

Study a daphnia through your hand lens or microscope

They're great to study because their transparent bodies allow you to see all their tiny internal bits and bobs throbbing and pulsing.

Get to know the inhabitants of your freshwater aquarium/wildlife pond

However, if you're planning on removing them from the tank to study, remember to be very, very gentle. Daphnia have feelings too!

Discover the age of a hedgerow

At one time there were no hedges in Britain. The first ones were planted by farmers who wanted to protect their crops and animals from bad weather and wild animals, and to stop them from running away (the animals, not the crops). Royal hunting forests were also enclosed by hedges so that kings and other assorted nobles could chase and slaughter wildlife to their hearts' content, sure in the knowledge that farmers' animals couldn't get in and the wildlife couldn't get out. Some hedges are hundreds of years old, so that matted tangle of green and brown you're looking at may well have been planted when Cromwell's Roundheads were bashing up Cavaliers.

I'm trying to plant a hedge!

If you want to discover how old a particular hedge is, this is how to do it.

1. Wander around the countryside until you spot a suitably old wild hedge. Choose a 30-metre (33 yard) length of it.

2. Count the number of different species of trees and shrubs you find in it. For instance, there might be hawthorn, ash and hazel in your stretch of hedge.

3. Multiply the number of species by 100. In this case 3 x 100, which gives you an age of 300 years for this particular hedge!

What are you doing in that hedge?

Plant a wild hedge

124

Hedges are incredibly important for wildlife because they provide long narrow hideaways for animals including birds, mice, rabbits, insects, voles and hedgehogs.

You're taking up all the room!

There used to be masses of hedges in the UK but after World War II farmers began ripping them out so they could use machines to farm larger areas. Recently, though, people have realised that hedges help support local wildlife and laws have been passed making it illegal to destroy them.

Do your bit by planting a wild hedge. Even a short one will be popular with all sorts of animals, especially if you plant a variety of hedgerow plants including hazel, holly, hawthorn, blackthorn, dog rose and dogwood, all of which have colourful flowers and berries, which attract many small mammals, birds, insects. The fallen leaves and long grass beneath your hedge will also provide shelter for wildlife.

Bark rubbing

The bark of some trees is smooth, while others are rough and cracked (and the bark of others is worse than their bite). Each sort of tree has its own unique bark pattern. You can discover the different textures by doing bark rubbings. Simply tape a thin piece of paper to the tree, unpeel a wax crayon and, with its long side, firmly rub the tree bark. You'll also discover that bark differs according to the age of a tree. For instance, the 'skin' of a young ash tree is smooth and unblemished (just like yours), while that of an old one will be wrinkled and gnarled (just like your dad's).

Knock me down with a feather!

Birds are the only animals which have feathers (apart from flying fish and dolphins). Feathers are made from the same stuff that our hair and fingernails are made from. If you run your finger down a feather you can 'unzip' its fibres then stroke it in the opposite direction and 'zip' them back up again. This is what birds do when they're preening. Birds replace their feathers by moulting (but not all at the same time).

You can pick up feathers from all sorts of places including fields, woods, parks, beaches, gardens (and duvets). A good way to display your feather collection is to get a piece of corrugated cardboard then fold it. Push the shafts of the feathers into holes then label them with a name and a small picture of the bird they came from next to it. You'll be tickled pink!

WARNING:

Feathers can have all sort of mites, bacteria and ticks in them, so always remember to wash your hands after touching them.

127 Bring a dragonfly back to life (well, almost!)

If you find a discarded dragonfly larva skin it will be quite dry and brittle. However, if you soak it gently in warm water it will soon become supple and life-like. You'll even be able to move that ferocious lower jaw as if it were still chomping on helpless tadpoles.

Overdone the moult a bit haven't you?

Do a bird beak survey

Birds beaks are adapted to the sort of food they eat.
Some have sharp beaks for spearing, some have hooked
beaks for cracking nuts, some have beaks which are
designed for shoveling. See how many sorts you can spot.

Now you see it, now you don't!
Watch some really wicked dragonfly action!

**Dragonflies are among the most exciting, talented and
spectacular of insects!**

They're brilliant flyers and would put the most high-tech
helicopter to shame, not only being able to hover, zoom upwards,
downwards, forwards, backwards *and* from side to side, but
to change speed and direction in a flash! They're also really
ferocious, snatching flies, midges, mosquitoes, butterflies, moths
(and unwary microlight pilots) out of the air and crunching them
up with their powerful jaws and teeth. The biggest dragonfly
wingspan ever measured was 2.5 feet. However, that was a
fossilised one – they've been flitting around planet earth for
300 million years! They also have great names, like the Black-
Tailed Skimmer, the Norfolk Hawker and the White-Faced Darter.

If you want to watch these magnificent flying assassins in action,
take your binoculars and a long stick to a pond or river on a sunny
late summer's day. Push the stick into the mud at the water's edge
so that it's leaning outwards then sit and wait patiently.

Dragonflies like high perches, so it's likely one will land on your
stick sooner or later. Then you can get a good look at it through
your binoculars. If you're lucky, one may actually land on you!

Go all bug-eyed. Get up close and personal with insects

Get out there and investigate some bugs. If you're lucky enough to have the use of a camera with a macro lens, i.e. a close-up lens, or a macro setting if it's a compact, you'll get some stunning shots. Here are some tips to help you spy and snap more successfully:

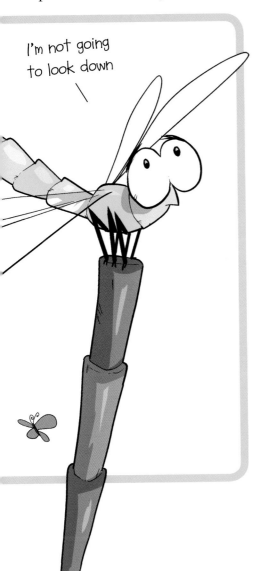

I'm not going to look down

Stand next to a plant that insects like to feed on. When they arrive, they'll simply assume you're part of the scenery.

Make sure you're on the same level as the bug, or even lower. If your bug's busy feeding, mating, cleaning (or filing its nails), it will take less notice of you.

If you go out early in the morning, insects are still a bit cold and dozy, so there's less chance of them flying away (or savaging you). Check out this insect pic-sharing website and get inspired...

www.flickr.com/groups/macro_insects_world/pool/

Give a caddisfly larva a 'make-over'

Caddisflies are moth-like creatures quite closely related to butterflies and moths. Their larvae develop underwater in ponds, lakes and streams. In order to camouflage themselves (or just because they're extremely vain) some types of caddisfly larvae make themselves little tubular outfits from tiny twigs, sand, gravel or plant stems which leave just their heads and legs sticking out. They do this by spinning a tube of silk and 'binding' their chosen material with it.

If you put a caddisfly in your aquarium and there are tiny stones in there, but no plants, sand or twigs, it will make its case from the tiny stones.

However, if you make sure there are no tiny stones, plants, sand or twigs in the tank, but you do put some very small, brightly coloured sequins in there, you'll be in for a surprise. In no time at all your creative little pet will begin fashioning itself a rather splendid bejeweled 'body-wrap' from the little sparklers!

Obviously, once you've seen your caddisfly do its bling thing, you should put some stones, plants or twigs in the tank so that it can revert to its normal camouflage if it wants to.

On the web

If you ever see a three-legged frog or toad it's because it had its leg bitten off by a dragonfly nymph when it was a tadpole. Watch the video 'nasty' here ...

www.news.bbc.co.uk/earth/hi/earth_news/newsid_8116000/8116692.stm

Bring up your own cannibals

Dragonflies are amongst the fiercest creatures known to aquatic folk, lurking in the muddy depths of ponds (and shopping precincts) as they wait to ambush their unsuspecting victims. Then, as soon as an unwary tadpole, insect or small fish comes near the nymph, it shoots out its lethal lower lip and stabs its prey, greedily drawing it back into its mouth and devouring it.

1. Using an aquarium (set up like the one you put together in activity 118) you can raise your own teenage tearaways – if you're hard enough!) Make sure your tank has plenty of weed and tiny pond creatures such as water fleas, bloodworms, lesser water boatmen and pond snail eggs, for your terrible teenagers to prey on.

2. Also, put in some large twigs sticking out of the water. Collect your nymphs from a pond using the dipping and trawling techniques you discovered in activities 28 and 29.

3. Once you've got them in the tank, put it in a shady outdoor spot. If you think no predators are likely to gobble your nymphs, leave the lid off.

You may have to wait some time for the nymphs to become adults. After hatching from an egg, dragonfly nymphs can spend from three months to three years in the water as they grow, going through a series of moults until they're ready to fly. You'll know when it's time for their final moult because they'll begin lurking near the surface of the water. Then, on the 'big day', they crawl up one of the twigs and begin to split their skin for the final time, emerging as a magnificent fully-fledged dragonfly.

Wild Things To Do With Butterflies

Track down some freshly laid, 'free-range' butterfly or moth eggs

Watch a butterfly or moth flitting around some weeds. When it settles, keep your eyes glued on the spot where it landed. Then, when it flies away, still staring intently at that particular spot, go over to it and examine the leaves for tiny, freshly laid, 'free-range' caterpillar eggs.

Once you've found some, snip the leaves off, taking care not to damage the eggs.

Remember what plant you found the eggs on. When your caterpillars hatch, this is exactly what they will want to eat!

Incubate your butterfly eggs

Once you've got your butterfly eggs, keep them in a lidded see-through container, (the sort that you buy squidgy washing machine 'blobs' in is ideal).

Make sure the eggs aren't being frazzled by bright sunlight and keep them moist by gently 'misting' them with water from a plant mister or even just by breathing on them!

Keep a close watch on the eggs. They could be hatching in just two or three days' time and you must be ready to devote your entire life to the upbringing of your new 'children'. (Well, ten minutes a day actually.)

Mother a moth

You can perform the activity [above] just as well with moth eggs, instead of butterflies. Why not do one and then the other, and observe the differences?

137 Coddle your caterpillars

When your caterpillars finally hatch they may be so small that you can hardly see them. It is more than likely that they will now eat their own egg cases, but once they've done that you will need to carefully transfer them to a new container, lined with damp tissue paper. The next step is to feed them. Give them fresh leaves, but not *too* fresh and not *too* old.

Change the leaves and tissue paper regularly – your youngsters will now be pooing quite enthusiastically and no one likes to live amongst piles of their own frass*, do they?

* frass: the naturalist's name for caterpillar poo.

138 Check out your caterpillars through your hand lens

Your caterpillars are actually nothing more than lots of little wandering stomachs - as you will now discover! Once you've got one under your hand lens, have a look at its various body bits.

Caterpillar care!

- Remember, the only safe way to move your caterpillars without hurting them is using a small soft paintbrush and a plastic spoon.
- Always wash your hands before handling your caterpillars to avoid contaminating them with bacterial infections.
- Never try to pull the caterpillars off a surface. They cling on very tightly and you might accidentally rip off their little legs.

Wild Things To Do With Butterflies

Transfer your caterpillars to a new home

When you see your little caterpillars growing and shedding their skins, it's time to gently transfer them to a bigger container. You should also feed them whole plants now, stem and all, rather than just leaves. Place the plants in small containers of water with tissue paper wrapped around the base to stop them from falling in and drowning. Also, check that there aren't any spiders in your caterpillar enclosure or you'll just end up with one really fat and happy spider.

Don't let go!
I'll get help

Pamper some pupae

After they've shed about five skins, your caterpillars will stop growing and begin to look like moody teenagers as they wander around looking for a suitable spot to pupate. Butterfly pupae like to dangle from twigs but moths will want some damp compost at the bottom of the container to bury themselves in. (Don't forget to sterilise the compost by microwaving for 10 minutes then leaving it to cool.)

You must now very carefully transfer your pupae, along with their twigs or compost, to a mesh cage, which they'll be able to flit around in when they finally emerge. This stage of their life will take some time, so you'll have to be patient.

Just remember to spray your pupae every few days with water using a plant mister to keep them moist. And stop feeding them! They're so busy concentrating on rebuilding their public image that they don't eat during this phase. What happens next is one of nature's best-ever party tricks. Inside the pupa, the caterpillar dissolves into a liquid mush then, quite gobsmackingly, rebuilds itself into a butterfly, moth (or small bi-plane).

Watch the final miracle take place

When you see your pupae going dark, then partly transparent, you'll know that the big day is nearly here. If you're lucky, you may witness the miracle of your butterfly or moth dragging itself out of its pupa, crawling up a plant stem and spreading its brand-new wings to dry out (then throwing back its head and letting out an awesome 'Cock-a-doodle-doo!'). This tends to happen at night, so check your pupae in the dark hours or early morning. Don't be disappointed if your 'new friend' looks a bit rubbish when it first appears. It needs time to get the blood pulsing around its body and to spruce itself up a bit before it becomes fully recognisable!

Wild Things To Do With Butterflies

142 Breed some more moths and butterflies

So that's it, you've successfully reared some little natural miracles. And now it's time to release them into the wild. However, you may wish to encourage your little captives to breed. This is easier with moths and many of them will mate in confined spaces, especially if you create the right conditions. For instance, a romantic candle-lit dinner for two – then again, perhaps not!

Butterflies need more flying space for breeding, so the greenhouse full of the butterfly-friendly plants you read about in activity 147 would be a perfect place.

143 Check out a Large White and learn to tell the difference

Large white butterflies are, you guessed it, large and white! They have black tips on their forewings and two black spots on the underside of their wings. Their caterpillars feed on cabbages and brussels-sprouts (and are really popular with vegetable gardeners). Learn to tell the different white butterflies that people call cabbage whites apart.

144 On the web

Check out these astonishing photographs of some very weird and wonderful caterpillars:

www.richard-seaman.com/Arthropods/Usa/Caterpillars/NorthernIllinois/index.html

Hunker down with some Holly Blues

These small bright blue butterflies have black spots on the underside of their wings and their caterpillars feed on two of the following things: ivy; pickled onions; old car tyres: holly; rotting underwear. Can you guess which they are? You can see them in April and May and then again in August and September. However, the ones you spot in August and September will be the children of the ones you saw earlier. The best places to spot them are hedgerows and gardens.

Make a marvellous moving caterpillar puppet

WHAT YOU NEED:

- A piece of A4 size paper
- Scissors
- A ruler and a pencil
- A glue stick
- 2 lolly sticks
- A small piece of card or paper
- Felt tipped pens or paint

WHAT TO DO:

Cut your A4 paper into 6 strips: If you measure 3.5 cm across the top and bottom this will divide the page into 6. You'll need to end up with 2 long strips, so now glue three pieces together long-ways twice.

Now glue together the two long strips at right angles to each other.

Fold the strips (still at right angles to each other) one at a time and keep folding so that it makes a 'concertina' shape – a bit like you sometimes see on Christmas decorations.

When you get to the end, glue the last bits together and trim off any extra paper. Now you have the caterpillar's body.

All you need to do is to attach lolly sticks to the front and back with glue to hold and move your puppet. Then make a head from cardboard and glue it to the front.

Don't forget to give your caterpillar some eyes – they have six on each side!), mandibles (jaws) for chomping through leaves, and antennae for smelling. You could also add legs.

Wild Things To Do With Butterflies

Wow! It's one of the brand new Holly Blue G2's!

147

'Say it with flowers' and bring a whole host of colourful characters flocking to your garden

If butterflies were people they'd spend their entire lives shopping for designer clothes and expensive perfume whilst guzzling sweets and fizzy drinks. And, at the first sign of rain or chilly weather, they'd make for the warmth and comfort of the nearest 5-star hotel. Yes, these flamboyant flappers are crazy for colour, addicted to intoxicating scents and absolute suckers for sweet nectar (the fuel that keeps them flying). They're also delicate creatures that don't like being cold or wet, or buffeted this way and that by strong winds.

If you want your garden to be aflutter with these lovely creatures, plant lots of brightly coloured, strongly scented flowers in a sunny and sheltered spot. Two flowers which are most likely to bring butterflies flocking to your garden are lovely fluorescent 'pink ice' plants, also called Sedums, and the tall, lavender-purple beauties known as Verbena.

It's not just the adult butterflies you've got to look after. Remember all those exotic airborne miracles were once humble caterpillars. So if you've got a few clumps of nettles in a forgotten corner of your garden, leave them for the caterpillars to feast on.

And, although an ivy-covered wall isn't a five-star hotel, it will certainly provide a sheltered place for adult butterflies to survive the winter.

Bleeurgh! This leaf is off!

148 Listen out for seasonal changes in birds' songs

Birds get really noisy in spring. However, they also sing at other times of year, but their 'tune' is different. For instance, in the autumn, the normally cheery song of the robin goes all sad and wistful. But then, around Christmas time, it perks up again (yes, they know Father Christmas is coming!). And blackbirds, who are so noisy in the spring spend the winter singing quietly to themselves in bushes and undergrowth.

Find a thrush's 'anvil'

Thrushes (and French people) love to eat snails. In order to get at them, they have to crack open the snails' shells by picking them up in their beaks and bashing them on stones or rocks. These stones are called 'anvils', after the implements blacksmiths beat metal on. You can spot a thrush's anvil by looking for the broken snail shells surrounding it.

150 Learn how to recognise birds in flight by drawing their outlines

You can copy flying bird silhouettes from birdwatching books or take your own photos of flying birds and copy them. As you draw, you'll immediately notice how birds' wings vary in shape. For instance, seagulls have narrow, long wings, rooks have deeply slotted ones and barn owls are round-winged.

Make an elastic band from dandelion sap

Warning! Don't do this one if you're allergic to rubber or latex (or dandelions).

Rubber is a natural material made from the milky sap-like fluid known as latex. We make all sorts of things from it including tyres, balloons, balls, erasers and rubber bands. But latex doesn't just come from rubber trees, it's found in ten per cent of all flowering plants. And one of these plants is the dandelion.

Collect some dandelion leaves and stems then break them up in order to squeeze out the milky sap. Now coat one of your fingers halfway down with the sap. Leave it for a while then gently roll off the dried sap. You now have your very own elastic band!

Make a home for a hedgehog

Turn a wooden box or crate upside down, make a hole for an entrance and cover it with stones, earth, wood (and some really tasteful wallpaper).

Hide your hedgehog house near a bank or hedge and make sure the entrance is facing south east or south if possible. Also make sure it's good and strong so that marauding badgers and foxes can't break in and eat 'Spike' and his/her family. Don't bother lining the box because Spike will do that as he/she prepares to settle in for the winter.

TIP:

Add a few stickle bricks for the little Spikelets to play with (optional).

Dandelions: turn wimps into superheroes!

For the activity after this one you'll need some super-strength. And, being high in calcium, potassium, and iron, dandelion leaves are just the thing to give it to you. Just pick some young leaves then wash them and boil them like spinach. Season to taste and enjoy!

WARNING!
The French call dandelion leaves 'pis-en-lit' which means 'wet the bed'. And it's true, they do make you want to go.

Make a bouncy ball from dandelion sap
WHAT TO DO:

1. Collect some dandelion leaves and stems then break them up in order to squeeze out the milky sap. When you have got half a teaspoon of sap, mix it with a quarter of a glass of water. Stir with a straw.

2. Now slowly add just a little drop of vinegar to make your latex stick together. Peel the latex off the straw and get rid of the excess water by squeezing it into a ball shape.

3. Using all that power you got from the dandelion leaves, bounce the ball! As it hits the ground it will change shape, absorbing the energy that propelled it downwards: a mixture of muscle power and gravity. Then, as the ball returns to its original shape, it releases that energy, which makes it bounce up again. Isn't nature wonderful!

Make a starter home for some 'first-time-flyers'

To see a couple of birds making their nest in a bird box that you've built is an incredibly thrilling and satisfying experience. And even *more* thrilling is to see the baby birds leaving the nest, having been successfully raised by their devoted parents!

Then, year after year, the birds will return to the box, making more and more babies (until you're waist-deep in baby blue tits and robins). As an added bonus, your nest box may well provide shelter for groups of birds on freezing winter nights!

WHAT YOU NEED:

- A plank of wood (15 cm (6 in) wide, 142.4 cm (56.1 in) long and 1.5 cm (0.6 in) thick) which has been treated with a preservative which is harmless to animals

- Another piece of wood (16 cm (6.3 in) x 4 cm (1.6 in) to attach your box to a tree or wall

- Glue

- Galvanised nails or screws

- A drill

- A brass hinge or piece of old inner tube from a bicycle

- A saw

- A grown-up to help you with the drilling, sawing, screwing and gluing (and to mend your cut fingers and squashed thumbs)

WHAT TO DO:

You must have put on weight since last year

1. Use a pencil and ruler to measure and mark out the plank.

2. Get your grown-up to cut out the sections with a saw.

3. Now decide on the size of entrance hole you're going to put in. Blue tits will need a 2.7 cm (1.1 in) hole, great tits a 3 cm (1.2 in) hole, and tree sparrows and nuthatches a 3.2 cm (1.3 in) hole. (Albatrosses will need a 3.2 metre (3.5 yard) hole).

4. Drill the hole in the front panel, making sure it's at least 12 cms (5 in) from the base of your bird box. If it's not, a determined cat could put its paw in, reach down and scoop out the baby birds.

5. Get your adult assistant to join the panels together with the nails or screws.

6. Attach the lid using the hinge or the piece of old inner tube.

7. Fix a catch to the lid to stop predators getting in. A piece of wire wound around two screw heads will do. Make some really small drainage holes in the bottom panel to allow the rainwater to drain out.

8. Fix the back panel to your bird box then nail it to a tree or wall high enough to stop cats reaching it. It's best to position your bird box so that it faces north-east or south-east. This will shield the entrance from strong sunlight and rain. Also, try to put it in a spot where you can watch the comings and goings of the birds.

Clean out your nest box

Your bird nesting box will be empty of visitors in the autumn. So clean out all the grot from it as it might be harbouring parasites which could infect next year's occupants.

Wild Things To Do With Ants

Confuse an ant

137

When ants find a good food source (or some good sauce) they leave a chemical trail to it, so that their mates will find their way to the goodies. When you see a line of ants following one of these trails, wipe part of it away with your finger, then observe how the ants are thrown into a state of confusion because they've suddenly lost their guideline.

Make an ant town

IMPORTANT NOTE!

Whilst working on this fascinating project, you must be careful that there are no gaps in your handiwork, or you will find hordes of totally berserk ants running amok in your living room, kitchen, bedroom (and pants).

WHAT YOU NEED:

- Plaster of Paris
- A jug
- A piece of plywood 30 cm x 30 cm (12 in x 12 in) square (this makes the base.)
- A sheet of hard clear plastic 28 cm x 28 cm (11 in x 11 in) – 6 wooden battens 2 cm x 2 cm (1 in x 1 in), of different lengths: 1 at 28 cm (11 in), 2 at 24 cm (9.5 in) and 3 at 10cm (4 in) long
- Clear rubber tubing 40 cm (16 in) long
- Modelling clay
- Garden soil
- A jam jar with a lid
- Black cloth or paper to cover your ant town
- Some duct tape

WHAT TO DO:

1. Screw all but the shortest batten flat against your base.
2. Lay the loose piece of wood in the centre.
3. Get creative with your modelling clay, making a network of corridors and little rooms no higher than the battens. Make sure that several of the corridors finish at the loose piece of wood. Fill the entrance with more clay then push your rubber tubing through the clay so that its end is right up against the other side of the loose piece of wood.
4. Mix your plaster of Paris then pour it into the gaps.

BTW:

You shouldn't have any ants in your ant town at this stage as mummifying them in plaster will defeat the object.

5. Leave the plaster to set for a couple of days, then remove the clay and the loose piece of wood. Put soil in the spaces where the modelling clay and loose piece of wood were.
6. Make a hole in the jam jar lid and push the other end of your tube through it, sealing any gaps with modelling clay. Now put your piece of clear plastic on top, sealing any gaps.
7. So that's it! You've built a magnificent formicarium. Now it's time to add the ants!

Comrades, we've reached a fork in the road

Wild Things To Do With Ants

Feed your ants
159

Now that your ants are established in ant town, start putting food into the jam jar. This can include ripe fruit, seeds, dead insects, small pieces of meat and the occasional little blob of honey or jam. You could also put some twigs covered with aphids in there and watch the ants 'milking' them for honeydew.

Stock your ant town
160

You must now go into the garden, park or local countryside armed with a trowel and a collecting box to put your new ants in. The best ants for your ant town are the little black, non-stinging ones which you will find under paving stones and pieces of wood.

Try to collect them in early spring when they are all clustered together. Ideally you should scoop out the entire colony including its queen, queen's daughters, (plus ugly sisters and wicked stepmother,) workers, pupae and eggs. You'll recognise the queen because she's loads bigger and fatter than all the other ants.

Carefully transfer the whole lot to the jar and add a blob of honey or cotton wool soaked in sugar water as a little welcoming treat for them. Leave the jar exposed to the light.

You don't have to be mad to eat ants – but it helps!

Watch your little guests make themselves at home

As most people know, next to having your head bitten off by a shark, moving house is one of the most stressful things that can happen to you. So, at first your ants will be all at sixes and sevens! However, after a while they'll calm themselves down and get busy organising their new home. **NB**: You must keep the ant town covered for most of the time as ants normally strut their stuff in darkness. However, every now and again you can lift up the black cloth or paper to see how they're doing.

You'll now be amazed to see that they've been busy turning the various 'rooms' into things like nurseries, food storage areas (multi-gyms and home theatres).

Lure ants from your house

Many people get rid of ants from their houses by finding their nests and pouring boiling water on them, which is a rather cruel and extreme way of preventing a few more adventurous members of the colony from entering their kitchen.

A better way to stop ants coming into houses is to locate the route which they take from their nest to your kitchen, then drop a blob of golden syrup, or something equally sweet and sugary, on it. The ants will soon find the syrup and will no doubt be delighted that it is so conveniently near their nest as it saves their little legs from getting tired as they walk the extra metres to your house.

Spread the good news about ants

Remind ant-mass murderers that ants do useful stuff like aerating the soil and destroying insect pests. They also provide food for birds, for instance the green woodpecker which eats about 2,000 ants a day.

Look for redwings and fieldfares in winter

These beautiful, colourful thrushes fly to Britain from Scandinavia and can be seen feeding on berries and fallen apples when the weather's at its coldest.

Photograph different ice patterns on a freezing cold day

Ice forms in all sorts of amazing shapes and patterns. If you go out quite early on a cold morning and look around, you'll soon realise that there's no such thing as 'ordinary' ice. For instance, look at the ice which is beginning to form at the edge of a stream, then compare it to the ice on windows, cars, ponds, frosted branches and plants. Or look for places where water splashes or drips, as they're often festooned with astonishing stalactite-shaped icicles.

And if you need further proof of the mind-boggling variety of 'ice patterns', just type those words into an internet image search. But be careful that you don't get carried away taking photographs of all these amazing shapes and patterns: mind you don't slip!

Great shot. Wow!

Look for hibernating butterflies in your garden shed in December

Brimstone, comma and small tortoiseshell butterflies hibernate in sheds, garages and log piles during the winter. If you find one enjoying its well-deserved mega-kip, take care not to disturb it.

Go birdwatching in winter

It's much easier to spot birds at this time of year. They haven't got all that summer foliage to hide behind!

Go wild animal tracking in the snow

The best time to find animal tracks is in the morning when the snow's still fresh and crisp.

Make a nature collage

Use natural things you've found. For instance, you could draw an oak tree full of birds, mammals and insects, then stick on some real bark and twigs, as well as real bird feathers and insects you've discovered on your travels. Or why not create a rock pool collage using real shells, sand and bits of seaweed.

Wild Things To Do With Tadpoles and Frogs

170 Get ahead – get a torch!

Frogs are really active at night doing stuff like hopping, snacking, swimming, croaking, mating (skateboarding and updating their Facebook profiles) while the rest of us are fast asleep. If you want to check out some fantastic frog action, the best thing to use is a head torch which will a) focus your attention on the frogs and b) leave your hands free to do stuff like crawling, using your camera (and having a really good scratch). Head torches are attached to a strap which fastens around your head like a miner's torch, and can be bought for just a few pounds.

Watch frogs making babies

Frogs hibernate during the winter, but as soon as the days begin to lengthen in February they wake up and eager little groups of them make their way to ponds in search of romance, glamour and excitement.

Some really enthusiastic males actually spend the winter in the ponds, hibernating in the mud on the bottom so that they'll be first on the scene when the party starts. As soon as the weather warms up, the frogs begin mating: the males wrap their legs around the females (whilst telling them they're not only the most beautiful, but the *wartiest* girl they've ever met!).

This goes on for several days and, after a while, clumps of fertilised spawn begin to appear around the edges of the pond.

Collect your frogspawn

Frogspawn looks like a lump of speckled jelly and you find it in shallow water.

Don't take your spawn from the wild. Wild ponds are already suffering because cities are getting bigger and pollution has increased. Try to avoid making life even harder for the frogs living in these wild ponds by stealing their children. It's a much better idea to take your 'frog-jelly' from garden ponds, especially ones that are really overcrowded with it.

Don't take too much spawn, otherwise your tank will soon become so overcrowded that your tadpoles will turn into 'madpoles' and begin eating each other. To collect the spawn, carefully scoop it into a plastic bag along with some pond water.

Prepare your tank

WHAT YOU NEED:

- A 10 litre (2-gallon) plastic tank
- Some water
- Gravel and pond plants, just like with your indoors/ outdoors freshwater aquarium (see page 66)
- A lid for your tank to make it cat, dog and baby-proof

I like to be early

Wild Things To Do With Tadpoles and Frogs

174 Introduce your spawn to the tank (and your parents)

When you get it home, don't just bung the spawn straight in the tank, as the shock of the sudden change in temperature will kill the unborn tadpoles. Instead, suspend your 'jelly-babies' on the surface of your aquarium, still in the plastic bag, for a few hours, adding some aquarium water to the bag every now and again. Once you're sure the temperatures are more or less equal, you can tip in the spawn.

And this one's Hugh, and Beth, and Tom, and...

Feeding your spawn

While you're raising your tadpoles, feel free to eat whatever you like: chocolate hobnobs, fish fingers, apples, chicken tikka masala... However, when it comes to feeding your *tadpoles*, that is an entirely different matter. You must pay careful attention to their diet, otherwise they'll quickly 'pop off to the great big pond in the sky' (scientific speak for 'die').

At first, there's no need to feed your 'jelly-babies', as they get their din-dins by absorbing their own egg yolk sacks. Then, when they finally break free they nibble the algae on the tank glass and feast on plants. After about three weeks, you can start feeding your tadpoles on tiny bits of boiled lettuce and rabbit food pellets.

Perhaps they ought to cut back on the rabbit food?

When your tadpoles develop their back legs they will become carnivorous (and therefore extremely dangerous). You can now begin feeding them on daphnia, bloodworms and flaked fish food.

When you notice that your tadpoles' tails are shrinking, cut down on the food as the absorbed tails will provide them with sufficient nourishment. However, as the tail does vanish, you can begin feeding them on small amounts of tiny insects such as greenfly and crickets.

WARNING!
Never overfeed your tadpoles. Uneaten food will rot and pollute the water.

Wild Things To Do With Tadpoles and Frogs

Keep your tadpoles clean

There's no need to actually bathe and shampoo your tadpoles individually, but do take care to keep their water extremely clean.

You do this by tipping away about half the water in the tank and replacing it with fresh pond water, rainwater or dechlorinated water every week (see page 68).

NB: After you've done the tipping away bit, you may find that your tadpoles have all disappeared. This is because you've just poured them all down the sink! To avoid this, tip the water into another container then use a net to fish out any taddies that have made a break for it. Another way to keep the tank clean is to pop in some pond snails, which will nibble away the algae (whilst also doing a bit of vacuuming and polishing).

177 Learn how to tell a frog from a toad

A lot of people find it hard to tell a frog from a toad – and even harder to tell a toad from a frog! Wrap your brain cells around this easy checklist, then impress your friends with your toadally stunning knowledge of these lookalike amphibians:

- A frog has smooth skin that feels moist.
- A toad has warty skin that feels dry.
- A frog's back is raised, with two ridges on either side.

Watch a miracle of nature take place before your eyes

At first your tadpoles will resemble nothing more than punctuation marks, starting out as full stops then quickly lengthening into tiny commas.

After they've broken free from their jelly, they'll attach themselves to weeds and the sides of the tank. If you examine them carefully at this stage you'll notice that they have developed the tiny feather-like gills that enable them to breathe underwater.

Then, their 'punctuation-mark' stage over, they will develop tails, which are soon followed by their legs. At this point, you'll see that their external gills gradually disappear, to be replaced by the internal ones, which you won't see. Next their front legs will begin to appear and their mouths and tongues will grow bigger. They'll also begin developing the big dopey-looking eyelids that you see on adult frogs.

Now into the last lap of their amazing metamorphosis, the tadpoles will begin to absorb their own tails. And with the disappearance of their tail they will become the little creatures known as froglets (or 'dinner' as grass snakes, blackbirds and ducks prefer to think of them).

IMPORTANT!

At this point you should get rid of most of the water in the tank, (leaving only about 5 cm (2 in) of water) and put in stones for the froglets to climb out onto.

- A frog's face is pointier than a toad's. Toads have rounder faces with more of a 'the light's on, but no-one's home' expression.
- Frogs have dark stripes around their legs. Toads' legs are spotty.
- Frogs jump using their strong back legs. Toads walk slowly.
- Frog tadpoles have pointed tails. Toad tadpoles have blunt tails.
- If you kiss a frog it will sometimes turn into a prince.
- If you kiss a toad it will always remain a toad.

Wild Things To Do With Tadpoles and Frogs

179 Say goodbye to your babies

Alas, it's now time to bid a tearful farewell to your little pals. Take them back to the pond where you first found them, and release your baby frogs into the wild. However, don't put them back into the exposed part of the pond as they'll be quickly snapped up by hungry predators.

Release them into weeds in the shallows or into any long grass next to the pond, to give them some cover.

Turn your tadpoles into piranhas!

Strip a skeleton by putting it in your tadpolearium. Any unfortunate recently deceased little creature will do: field mouse, vole, or shrew, for example. The little monsters will nibble the flesh from the bones, revealing the skeleton in all its glory. But don't forget to keep freshening up the water, as in activity 119.

NB: Only works on smallish skeletons – so it's totally unsuitable for big skeletons, like deer, eagles, wild boar, or woolly mammoths.

Free at last!

Keep a tadpole diary

All the best naturalists record the astounding things they see. Record the day-to-day progress of your little pals using sketches, photographs and notes.

_____

_____

_____

_____

_____

_____

_____

_____

_____

_____

_____

_____

Stick your photos here

Discover the weird world of Oak Marbles, Robin's Pincushions and Witches Brooms

All of these are rather romantic, old country names for very *unromantic* and very weird plant mutations known as 'galls'. Galls are caused by parasites, (such as insects, fungi and bacteria), invading a plant then causing its cells to get much bigger, or to multiply really rapidly. An Oak Marble gall is caused by a wasp called Andricus kollari ('Andy' to his mates). This wasp lays its eggs in the oak tree, and, when its larvae hatch, the very fact that they are there stimulates the tree to produce the marble galls. The larvae live inside the marble galls and eat them. (Yes, the 'gall' of it!)

Discover the secret interior of a gall

Get your adult to dissect the gall so you can see the little homes those pesky parasites have made. All will be revealed!

WHAT YOU NEED:

- A sharp knife
- A gall
- An adult

Leaf assassin

Catch a falling leaf before it hits the ground. (It's harder than you'd think!)

Grow a gigantic pumpkin or marrow

Buy a marrow or a pumpkin plant or grow one from seed. In June plant it in a sunny spot in some compost mixed with some well-rotted horse or cow manure. Water it regularly, talk to it nicely and be amazed as it turns into a giant.

Robin's Pincushion is caused by a wasp, too, but this one lays its eggs on wild roses. Witches Broom is found high up in birch trees. It's caused by a fungus that stimulates the galls to grow, then feeds on them. In the old days, country people believed that these galls were real witches' brooms (poor, deluded twits).

Why not make a collection of different galls?

How galling! —

Press flowers and leaves the easy way

WHAT YOU NEED:

- An old telephone directory or some other sort of old, heavy book
- Something quite heavy such as a metal weight, a housebrick (or St Paul's Cathedral)
- Some leaves and flowers

WHAT TO DO:
Put the leaves and flowers in the middle of the big book and close it. Put the weight on top and leave it for a few weeks then 'hey *pressto!*' they'll be flat! You can now display your pressed flowers in albums, picture frames or use them to make greetings cards

Important note: always press leaves and flowers when they're freshly picked.

Make a 'Buzz Stop' (a starter home for bumblebees)

Bumblebees (or 'Dumbledores', as they were once known) are those big furry orange-and-black ones which come out as soon as the weather gets warm.

Bit s'warm – isn't it?

These early bees are queens who are looking for somewhere suitably palatial to bring up their children, such as a disused vole hole. Save them the trouble of all that tiring house-hunting by providing them with a ready-made subterranean starter home. Unlike honey bees, bumblebees only build small nests so there's no chance of them gathering in huge great swarms and frightening the cat to death.

WHAT YOU NEED:
- A plant pot with a drainage hole in the bottom
- Four small stones or corks
- A piece of wood or slate about 5 cm x 5 cm (2 in x 2 in)
- Some sawdust or wood shavings

WHAT TO DO:
Dig a hole in the ground so that your plant pot will fit in it upside down. Fill the hole with the sawdust and wood shavings. Put the plant pot in it so that the drainage hole is level with the surface of the ground. Put some stones on the soil around the edge of the plant pot. Place the piece of wood or slate on the stones, leaving just enough room for a bumblebee to crawl under it. Put a notice outside advertising the vacant 'property'.

WARNING!
No matter how cute they look, never cuddle a bumble bee.

Make a bee box (or a wasp wrestle)

These are ideal for the 'No-Mates-Nigel' insects known as solitary bees. These slightly sad and stand-offish insects don't live in communities like honey bees and bumblebees, but prefer to squat in stems and holes hollowed out by boring beetles.

WHAT YOU NEED:

- A plant pot. Some wire or string
- Drinking straws, hollow plant stems or thin bamboo canes
- Scissors

Why yes, I'm a boring beetle – How did you know?

To Let
Residents must beehive

WHAT TO DO:

Put the straws or bamboo canes in the plant pot then trim them so they are level with the top of the pot. Attach the pot to a south-facing tree trunk with the wire, so that it's got a nice sunny outlook. You should soon see bees investigating the empty property and weighing up whether it suits their requirements (good local schools, handy for the shops, that sort of thing) then making their homes in the straws or canes, as they enthusiastically refurbish them with some top-of-the-range designer mud.

Make a proper flower press

WHAT YOU NEED:

- 2 pieces of thin scrap wood such as plywood
- Around 10 pieces of cardboard
- Around 20 pieces of water colour or blotting paper
- 4 wing nuts with washers
- 4 screw bolts about 20cm (8 in) long
- A drill and drill bit which matches the diameter of the screw bolts
- A pencil
- A grown-up to do the drilling

WHAT TO DO:

1. Cut both pieces of wood to the size you want. Think about the size of the plants you want to press in your flower press. 30 cm x 30 cm (12 in x 12 in) or smaller is probably about the ideal size (however if you want to press giant sunflowers it'll need to be a bit bigger).

NEW!
SILVERFISH FOOD

CONTAINS:
SCRAPS OF PAPER
GLUE
SPILLED FOOD

Yum!

Press some seaweed

Use your flower press to press some seaweed. Put the seaweed on a piece of paper in a tray of water and arrange it into a suitably artistic shape then slide the seaweed and paper out of the tray and transfer it to the press.

FASCINATING FACT!

Because it's so good at slithering along long, tight tunnels, the tamer cousin of stoats and weasels, the ferret, was used by the Boeing aircraft company to wire their enormous passenger jets.

2. Drill a hole at each of the four corners of your pieces of wood making sure they will be in line when placed together.

3. Trim the pieces of cardboard and blotting paper to the same size as the wood. Trim off their corners to avoid the screws.

4. Place one piece of card then two pieces of blotting paper alternately, in as many layers as you please (but stop when your flower press reaches the ceiling).

5. Place your flower and leaf specimens between the sheets of blotting paper.

6. Thread the screws through the holes from beneath and tighten with the wing nuts to press the flowers.

WARNING:
As you tighten the wing nuts don't be surprised to hear the flowers and leaves whimpering pitifully (you heartless monster, you!)

Spy on a silverfish!

Tip-toe into your kitchen at a quiet time, such as early morning or late at night and you may well spot some silverfish, or carpet-sharks, as they're also known. You'll know when you see a silverfish as it really does look and move as if it's 'swimming' around, wiggling and shimmying its way over your cupboards and worktops. Silverfish eat scraps of paper, glue and spilled food.

Watch a woolly bear

192

Carpet beetles live in things made from natural materials including curtains, fur coats ... and carpets! Their larvae are known as 'woolly bears'. If you spot one, you'll realise why!

ROAR!

Wild Things To Do With Moths

193 White as a sheet

Attract moths by stringing up a large white sheet between two trees then putting a light above it. Remember to get up early though or the birds will have eaten the moths before you get a chance to inspect your 'collection'.

194 Pamper some pupae part 2

If you're a bit lazy and don't want to bother with the egg or caterpillar part of breeding moths (see page 81), you can just buy the pupae. And failing that, (if you're a *total* slacker), why not miss out the pupae bit too, forget the whole thing and just watch TV!

Can you stop that? – I'm trying to read

Bring out the 'night shift!'

Sadly, there are only 60 types of butterfly left in the UK. But there are still more than 2,500 sorts of moth. And by no means are they all the dull brown things that fly out of skinflints' wallets and whose caterpillars chew holes in socks. They come in a huge variety of fascinating shapes and colours. And they're just as addicted to sweet sticky stuff as butterflies. So a great way to bring them flittering and swooping into your garden on a summer's night is to mix up some Moth Candy, a concoction of sugary ingredients they won't be able to resist.

WHAT YOU NEED:

- A big pan
- A jar
- A spoon
- A thick paintbrush
- A torch
- Some brown sugar
- Treacle
- Fruit juice
- Water and cola
- An adult to help with the mixing and heating

WHAT TO DO:

1. Add all the ingredients to the pan and put it on a low heat, stirring it constantly and adding more water if it looks like sticking. Keep stirring until everything has dissolved (apart from the pan) and the Moth Candy has the consistency of really thick, gooey paint.

2. When it's cooled a little, pour it into your jar, take it out into the garden and begin daubing it on various things around the garden including tree trunks, shed walls and fence posts (but not the cat).

3. When it's dark, go out with your torch and check out the moths (whilst resisting the temptation to lick the fence posts).

Wild Things To Do With Moths

Look on lime, poplar and willow tree bark for lime hawkmoths

You can fine these lovely little creatures in May and June. They're a gorgeous pink and green colour with superbly 'scalloped' wings.

Unearth some genuine hidden treasures

In the autumn, take a trowel or hand fork and gently start exploring the earth around the base of trees such as willows or poplars. Don't dig deeper than 10 cm (4 in). What you're looking for are the reddish brown pupae of moths.

Check out some pictures online so that you know what you're looking for. When you've found them, put them in a seed tray of sterilised compost (heated in the microwave for 10 minutes, then left to cool JUST the compost – not the moths silly!) and keep them somewhere cool (e.g. Disneyland).

Make a wine rope for the moths

This is similar to the Moth Candy (but it also gets the moths really squiffy). Just like before, you'll need a tame adult to help you. Put a kilogram of sugar and bottle of cheap red wine in your pan, over a low heat, and stir the sugar until it has dissolved. Let the wine mixture cool then dip ropes, bits of string and lengths of cloth into it. Finally, hang them from tree branches (along with some crisps, cheese on sticks and olives) and watch the moths tuck in.

Trip the light fantastic

If you've got to get up early for school and don't want to wander round your garden like a moth-hungry vampire, you can attract moths straight into your house. Simply leave the window open and the light on until midnight on a summer night.

This works best in the bathroom, because there are fewer places for the moths to hide, and more chance of you spotting them! In the morning, you'll be rewarded by the sight of lots of little living works of art all hanging around your bathroom. Record them by sketching them and photographing them and writing down their names in your nature notebook.

FASCINATING FACTS!

Chinese Character moths look exactly like little dollops of bird poo. And who'd want to eat that! Scientist have identified 200,000 types of moths around the world but believe there are probably five times that many flitting around the planet. The Hummingbird Hawkmoth's tongue is longer than its entire body. Imagine that in a human! Moths navigate by using the moon and stars or the earth's magnetic field. The Cecropia moth can smell a mate from 7 miles away.

I'm a mam-moth!

Make an 'en-suite' bird bath

Just like us humans, birds need to take a bath every now and again. They also need to have a drink at least twice a day, so by making them a bird bath you will also provide them with somewhere to 'wet their whistles'. You can make a bird bath from all sorts of shallow containers including seed trays, plant pot saucers and dustbin lids.

Make sure they have a rough surface inside so that the birds don't slip while they're splashing around. Also put a stone in the bath so that any small animal that happens to fall in can climb out again. It's also a good idea to position the bath on top of some sort of stand so birds can keep an eye out for marauding cats.

If you don't want to make a bird bath, you can buy ready-made ones which come with all sorts of extras including pedestals, fancy decorations (soap racks, shower attachments...). Also, if you visit car-boot sales, you can pick up some very nice old-fashioned bird baths. However, if you do buy a second-hand bird bath, clean it thoroughly before putting it out for the birds. Put your bird bath in a shady site, as bright sunlight will soon dry up the water. Fill it with clean, fresh water, keep it topped up and clean it every few weeks to prevent the spread of disease.

Watch birds bathing

Unlike humans, birds will not mind one bit if you watch them as they take their bath. For some reason, birds get very carried away when they bathe and will often frolic quite excitedly once they're in the water. Then, as soon as their feathers are good and wet, they'll begin to preen themselves.

Preening is something which is mainly done by birds (and self-obsessed celebrities), which involves them carefully rearranging their feathers as they spread oil from their 'preen gland', so that they remain waterproof with an insulating layer of air trapped underneath their feathers to keep them warm.

'Sall right, false alarm

FASCINATING FACTS!

In three weeks of feeding their chicks, the average pair of great tits will bring them 8,000 caterpillars and other insects.

Go foraging for some funky fungi

When October and November come around it's time to go down to the woods, where you'll be in for a big surprise! All sorts of fantastic fungi appear in the autumn, with equally fantastic names like King Alfred's Cakes, Ear fungus, Orange Peel, Fly Agarics, Lawyers' Wigs, Puffballs, Beefsteaks and the extremely funky, Stinkhorns! Wonder at them, photograph them and draw them – but DON'T touch them!

Explode a giant puffball

You can find these round, white fungi in fields between July and November and they are sometimes as big as a football. If you poke them with a stick you'll see them 'exploding' throwing out great clouds of white spores. Very spectacular!

DO NOT TOUCH THE MUSHROOMS

Make a funky fungi print

Fungi, such as mushrooms and toadstools, reproduce themselves by dropping tiny 'spores' which the wind distributes to new places for them to grow.

This activity is a way of spotting the spores. All you need is a mushroom or a toadstool.

WHAT YOU NEED:
- A mushroom or a toadstool
- A plastic bowl
- Hairspray
- Some coloured card

WHAT TO DO:

Discard the stalk and place your mushroom on the card with the underside down. Cover it with the bowl. Leave it for a day then carefully remove the bowl and lift the mushroom off the card to reveal the pattern made from the spores that have fallen from the mushroom. Spray your 'print' with the hairspray to fix it on the card and stop it smudging.

Listen out for starling mimics

Starlings are brilliant at imitating other sounds. Listen out for their amazing impressions of things like telephones, car alarms and reversing trucks.

Starlings also imitate cat miaows, dog barks, music and human voices. Mozart, the famous composer, had a pet starling which learned to whistle part of one of his piano concertos. When the starling died he gave it a special funeral where heavily-veiled mourners marched in procession, sang hymns and listened to Mozart recite a poem he had written in honour of his dead pet.

Wild Things To Do With Worms

MOST IMPORTANT ANIMAL

Investigate earthworms

Earthworms are fascinating and incredibly useful creatures which have been tunneling, burrowing and chomping their way through the surface of the Earth for the last 120 million years or so.

Aristotle, the Greek philosopher (384 BC – 322 BC), described earthworms as the 'intestines of the earth', because they improve the soil by aerating it and digesting dead and decaying matter like leaves and ex-animals, which then turn into humus. Humus is the magical stuff that not only fills the soil with the nutrients which plants are so dependent upon, but also allows it to retain the water that all plants rely on for healthy growth. And without those juicy, tasty plants to eat, not much else on this planet would survive.

An acre of grassland can contain as many as three million worms, all busily doing their bit for the environment as they dig out nearly 3,000 miles (4800 km) of burrows and munch their way through 5 tonnes of soil every single year. So, what are you waiting for? Logon and learn even more about earthworms here:

www.kids.nationalgeographic.com/kids/animals/
creaturefeature/earthworms/

Watch worms at night

Earthworms are nocturnal, so your best chance of observing them 'in the wild' is at night. They are also unable to see the colour red, so you can get a good night-time view of them by using a torch covered with clear red plastic such as a sweet wrapper.

Charm some earthworms

Imaginative, (but useless) worm charming for 'free-spirited' types:

1. Put a worm in a basket then, wearing an appropriately ridiculous hat, take a flute or school recorder and play it at the worm in the hope that it will rise up, waggle its head from side to side and spit viciously in a suitably dramatic cobra-like fashion.

Really successful worm charming techniques for 'down-to-earth' types:

1. 'Grunting': Don't worry, you don't have to grunt – although if you feel like doing a bit of undignified snorting, please feel free. First, drive a wooden stake into the ground – this is your 'stob'. Next, take a piece of metal, known as your 'rooping iron', and rub it across the top of the stake. Now be amazed as dozens of worms begin to emerge from the earth, casting panic-stricken glances this way and that.

2. 'Twanging': This simply involves pushing a garden fork into the ground then hitting it with a stick (the fork, not the ground).

But not TOO damp!

TOP TIP!

Charm your worms from damp ground. They tend not to hang around in really dry earth as it makes slithering very difficult. You'll recognise 'fertile' earthworm territory because it will be dotted with the wiggly little heaps of worm poo known as casts.

Wild Things To Do With Worms

Discover how worm charming works

209

Read about the incredible worm charming techniques, and try them out for yourself…

THEORY 1:

Charles Darwin, amongst others, came to the conclusion that the vibrations caused by the 'twanging' sound just like the noises made by approaching moles. Moles are worms' number one enemies, and the greedy little burrowers eat their own weight in the wriggly creatures every day. So, at the merest hint of nearby mole activity, worms immediately head for the surface in the hope that they can escape their furry predators.

THEORY 2:

Worms mistake the vibrations caused by the 'grunting' for the sound of rain pitter-pattering on the earth above them. Some people think the worms are terrified of being drowned in their underground tunnels and that's why they rush to the surface.

GRUESOME FACT

When a mole eats a worm, it first uses its paws to squeeze all the soil and muck out of its gut, rather like us squeezing the last bit of toothpaste out of a tube.

What have I told you about squeezing your worm?

Organise a worm charming competition

Worm charming is now an international sport. On June 29, 2009 a 10-year-old British girl called Sophie Smith set the current world record by charming 567 worms during Britain's World Worm Charming Championship.

THE RULES:

1. The area from which you charm your worms should be no larger than 3 m by 3 m (10 ft x 10 ft).

2. All charmers are allowed a five-minute warm up (or 'worm-up').

3. A worm charming team consists of the charmer, the catcher and a third person who's job it is to count the worms.

4. All worms must be returned to the ground after the contest. It's your duty as a conscientious naturalist and environmentalist.

ANOTHER GRUESOME FACT

Moles don't always eat worms the moment they catch them. Sometimes they simply immobilise them with toxic spit and stash them in a sort of underground 'worm-flesh warehouse', which might contain as many as 1000 paralysed worms.

Discover how an earthworm moves

Put one of your earthworms in a transparent container with some moist soil in it to make it feel at home. Now look closely at your worm. You'll notice that its body is made up of lots of segments which look a bit like very small joined-up tyres.

Watch carefully and you'll see that your worm's body contracts and relaxes, enabling it to move along a surface. It does this using its muscles. First it will use them to make itself long and thin. Once it's done that, it secures its front end by sticking its tiny bristles called setae in the soil. Now it pulls its rear end forward. This makes the worm short and thick. Once the rear end is in place, your worm will withdraw its front 'setae' from the soil, whilst digging its rear 'setae' in. Now that its rear end is anchored it can thrust its front end forward, making itself long and thin again. Then the whole process is repeated.

Wild Things To Do With Worms

Squash an earthworm (well, a balloon actually)

One of the reasons earthworms are able to tunnel so well is that their bodies are 70–95 per cent water (all depending on how desperate they are for a wee). This makes them very flexible. This activity is a great way of understanding what that means. Fill up a sausage-shaped balloon with water almost to the top, tie it up, then try squidging it. You'll find that as you squash one part of the balloon the water moves to a different bit. Which is why earthworms never get stuck in tight spaces, no matter how fat they are!

Make a worm observation station a.k.a. a wormery

Charles Darwin kept worms in tanks in his billiards room and studied them for 39 years. Some of his experiments involved him breathing on them while chewing tobacco or cotton wool soaked in vinegar, in order to test their sense of smell. He proved that they have no sense of hearing by shouting at them and playing the bassoon to them. He also tried to find out how intelligent they were.

WHAT YOU NEED:
- A large, clean, plastic jar
- Some black paper or dark-coloured cloth
- A cool, dark cupboard
- Clingfilm
- Some moist soil of different varieties
- Top layer materials, such as old leaves, vegetable peelings, tea leaves and overripe fruit.
- And, of course, some earthworms!

WHAT TO DO:

1. Once you've got your wormery jar sorted, fill it with layers of soil of different colours and textures. For instance: sieved garden soil, peat, fine sand, chalky soil and a thin layer of gravel. Each layer should be about 1 cm (0.5 in) deep and covered with your final top layer.

2. Leave about 5 cm (2 in) of space at the top of your jar. Now add some water. (Not too much though, it's a wormery, not a fish tank!)

3. Put in your worms and stretch the clingfilm over

We're not coming out

the top, pierce a few air holes in it, then cover your wormery with a dark-coloured cloth or black paper and put it in the cupboard. Every few days, uncover your wormery to find out what your worms have been up to and check that the soil is damp.

Where's this giant worm then?

FASCINATING FACT!

The biggest earthworm in the world is the Giant African Earthworm. This huge creature can grow to be as long as 6.7 m (22 ft) and weigh over 1.5 kg. You'd need a very big wormery to keep a bunch of these!

Your early morning 'wake-up-call!' Get completely 'tabsmacked' by the dawn chorus

The sound of hundreds of birds twittering, trilling and cheeping for all they're worth at daybreak is one of nature's miracles. Human beings have been hearing this awe-inspiring symphony of birdsong for thousands of years. Every morning, starting in March, all sorts of birds leap out of bed before it's even light and begin singing their little hearts out. It starts with just a few birds, like the robin, wren and blackbird, with more and more birds joining in until, when its fully light, there is a tumult of bird sound which goes on for at least another forty minutes. But the birds aren't just tweeting because they enjoy a good old singsong. It's mainly the male birds that are doing the singing and they're doing so to a) stake out their territory and b) to attract a mate.

This spot's taken

Record the dawn chorus

The dawn chorus is at its peak at the end of April and beginning of May, when summer visitors such as chiffchaffs and nightingales join in the mass singsong. To record the dawn chorus, you'll have to get up at about 4.30 am, then get into position with your recording equipment. There are all sorts of recording machines available, ranging from inexpensive digital ones to the state-of-the-art stuff that professionals use. Check out your mobile phone as that may make the perfect recording device.

This activity is well worth the effort! You can listen to your recording on the darkest and most miserable of winter days and be instantly transported to that glorious spring morning when you first made it.

Go completely wild in a flower meadow

Learn the names of 30 wild flowers then try and identify them while you're out walking in the countryside.

TOP TIP!

• Get used to your recording equipment beforehand, so that when you're out in your garden or the local park, you're not fiddling with dials and buttons and missing out on the sounds.

• Choose your microphone position carefully so that it picks up as much birdsong as possible, ideally it should be surrounded by birds.

• Make yourself inconspicuous, perhaps by using the hide you made in activity 13 (see page 12).

Listen for the song thrush in January

In the New Year male song thrushes start staking out their territory by singing their lovely liquid-sounding song with its enchanting repeated phrases. Check out this video so you know what to listen out for.

www.youtube.com/ watch?v=X3kPcalAEi8

Test the strength of an egg's inner membrane

Put an egg in a bowl of vinegar and see what happens. After ten minutes, you'll see bubbles of gas forming on the eggshell. Leave the egg overnight, and you'll see that the vinegar has dissolved the whole of the eggshell, leaving just the egg membrane, which is there to protect the chick.

Learn birdsongs in March

This is a really good time to pick out different sorts of birdsong because the summer visitors haven't arrived yet. This means there isn't the absolutely confusing hubbub of song you hear in May.

Listen to tawny owls hooting in October

Lots of people think tawny owls go 'twit twoo'. But if you listen carefully what you'll hear is actually more of a 'ke-wick' sound followed by 'hoo-hoo-hooo'. The 'ke-wick' sound is made by a female tawny owl and the hoo-hoo-hooo' is the male tawny owl answering her. This totally spooky duet will make the hairs on the back of your neck stand on end! Check out this blood-chilling link.

www.rspb.org.uk/wildlife/birdguide

Draw a picture on an egg

If you draw a picture or write your name on the shell using the rubber solution that is used for mending bycicle punctures, it will protect the shell from the vinegar. Once you've done this, immerse the egg in vinegar, leave it overnight and see what happens.

Test the strength of eggshells

Chicken eggshells are really fragile. But they're also really strong! They have to be in order to protect the very fragile baby birds that grow inside them. Balance four eggs, small end down on four bottle caps then lay a wooden board across them. Now begin piling books on top of the eggs. You'll be amazed at how many they can support! Now try it with the eggs balanced on their sides. **NB**: don't try this with other eggs.

Protect your garden wildlife from cats

Pet cats kill lots of wild creatures (and postmen). To reduce the risk of this happening, give your cat a big noisy quick-release collar bell so that the birds know when it's around. Keep neighbours' cats out of your garden by making your fences and hedges moggy-proof and position your wildlife feeding areas so that creatures can spot prowling predators before they pounce.

224
Become an owl pellet detective

FIND YOUR EVIDENCE

Most owls hunt in the dark and will often bump off three or four little creatures such as shrews, voles or mice, in a single night, not to mention the occasional worm, beetle, frog, bird (or lost child).

Rather than daintily picking out the tastiest bits of their victims, they usually gulp them down in one go. Or, if their prey is too large to swallow whole, for instance a rat (or blue whale), they first pull it apart with their beak. Like all birds, owls are unable to chew, so their supper passes first to their gizzard then to their stomach. However, the indigestible bits of the prey like fur, teeth, feathers, bones (and children's shoes) will remain in the owl's gizzard, which is another sort of stomach specially designed for storing all this grot.

Of course, the owl can't store bones and feathers in its gizzard indefinitely. So, a few hours after dinner, it sits at its favourite roosting spot and regurgitates a 'pellet' of undigested bits and pieces.

You can find these owl pellets beneath roosting places such as big trees and disused buildings, where you'll also see masses of huge white splatters which are the owls' droppings.

FASCINATING FACTS!

Owls can only move their eyeballs a tiny fraction, so to look around them, they have to swizzle their entire heads. A tawny owl can twizzle its head almost all the way around, so if you sneak up on it, it will clock you without even moving its body.

EXAMINE THE CLUES

Once you've got your pellet, soak it in some mild disinfectant. Then you're ready to sketch or photograph it. First pull it apart to discover the victims' identities. One way to do this is to break it up and then soak the lumps in a jar of warm water for a few hours. After that you can shake the jar gently so that the fur or feathers float to the top. Pour the water through a sieve, pick the bones out and soak them again. Keep doing this until you end up with a collection of skulls, jaws, teeth, vertebrae, and limb bones. Now comes the challenge. You must identify and then match the different bits of evidence, grouping your bones according to their previous owners.

Another way to dissect your owl pellet is to keep it dry and pull it apart with tweezers and a needle.

PRESENT YOUR EVIDENCE

Once you've got all the sad little victims' skeletons sorted, cleaned and dried you can display them by gluing them to some black card and labelling them alongside your picture of the owl pellet. Gruesome...

225

'Enlighten' some little creatures with a Tullgren funnel

Some tiny creatures are so determined to remain hidden in leaf litter or soil that you have to flush them out with a device known as a Tullgren funnel (after its inventor, Mr Funnel).

WHAT TO DO:

WHAT YOU NEED:

- The top half of a big plastic drinks bottle – this will be your 'funnel'
- Some wire mesh
- Wire cutters or tin snips
- A 'grown-up' to do the snipping
- A large jar to stand your funnel in
- An adjustable table lamp
- A white plastic lid

1. Get your grown-up to snip a circular shape from the wire mesh – just big enough to fit snugly about three-quarters of the way down your cut bottle.

2. Turn the bottle upside down, fit the mesh into it and place it in the bucket. You now have your funnel.

3. Now cover the top with freshly collected leaf litter or soil. Position the lamp so the bulb shines down onto the leaf litter, then switch it on. **NB**: Make sure the lamp is not too near the leaf litter, you only want to look at the mini-beasts, not *barbecue* them!

4. Leave the funnel for about an hour, then lift it up to see what little creatures have fallen into your jar. The heat from the lamp should have made the creatures so uncomfortable that they want to escape from the leaf litter. Their natural instinct is to climb upwards but they

are so disturbed by the lightbulb (having mistaken it for the enormous eye of some monstrous alien creepy crawly from outer space), that they scuttle downwards and fall into the bucket.

Once you have your specimens in the bucket, transfer them to your lid so that you can examine them through a magnifying glass or microscope. Don't be surprised if you discover some animals that are entirely new to you.

Once you've examined your catch, return it to its natural habitat whilst apologising to the poor little things for frightening the 'living daylights' out of them!

Make a record of your growing levels

Draw around your hand and write the date next to the drawing. Wait a few weeks or months then do it again and see how your hand has grown and changed shape.
NB: if you notice that you've got more fingers than the last time, consult your doctor immediately!

WHAT YOU NEED:
• a pencil
• a drawing book (size A4)

Inside the outline of your hands, you could also note down a few other things you did with them around the time you drew round them e.g. stroked a moth, did brain surgery on a carrot etc.

Watch a slug slither

Imagine having just one foot with a special gland in it that squirts out masses of slime. Well, that's what snails and slugs travel around on.

All right, it's not *quite* a skateboard, but it does work very successfully. To move, slugs and snails use their muscles to make a rippling motion, which passes along the length of the 'sole' of their foot, enabling them to push against whatever surface they happen to be on. You can watch the 'ripple effect' in close-up simply by putting a slug or snail on a piece of damp glass or perspex. A glass coffee table would be perfect!

Then, once your slug gets going, lift up the glass or get under the coffee table and enjoy this 'really moving' experience. And just to make things happen more smoothly, they squirt oodles of slime out. This ensures that they can slide around quite comfortably, no matter how rough the going gets (and, if they run out of slime, they just hop).

The slime is so sticky that slugs and snails can climb walls, cling to plants and hang upside down from ceilings.

Make a house for a mouse

Either split an old tennis ball or make a hole in it. Put it in some long grass or attach it to a cane stuck in long grass in order to attract harvest mice.

Do a litter pick

But make sure you wear thick gardening gloves to do it!

Make a 'boot-scraping' garden

Like other animals, human beings are seed distributors. To discover just how many future wild plants you're carrying from place to place, follow these instructions! The first step is to get your adult to sterilise a tray of compost by heating it in a microwave oven for 10 minutes. Then, when you get back from a country walk, scrape the mud from your boots onto the compost. Keep your little compost-tray garden in a sunny spot, watering it well, and you'll soon be amazed to see just how many plants-to-be you were carrying around with you.

Leave out nest-making material for birds

In the spring, you can help birds with their nest building by putting out nesting materials such as sheep's wool, knitting wool, bits of felt, feathers, dry grass, soft tufty bits of Pampas grass, hay and even your own hair! But don't cut it off especially…)

Hang the materials on twigs and branches or in a plant pot so that the birds can collect it easily.

Get to grips with a 'scorpion'!

MISSION: To discover some pseudo-scorpions!

Add leaf litter and soil to your funnel (see pages 130–131) whilst noting all the fascinating little wrigglers and squigglers which turn up. Sooner or later you will come across some pseudo-scorpions. These charming little creatures have vicious-looking pincers and inject their victims with a sort of digestive venom which turns their insides into a gloopy mush which the pseudo-scorpions then suck out... Yum yum!

Actually, pseudo-scorpions aren't real scorpions. They only look like them. And they're only about 2 mm (0.07 in) long. So, unless you're very small and extremely timid, there's no need to be afraid of them.

Spy on nesting birds

All you need for this is your binoculars, a notebook and a little bit of patience.

In the spring you'll see birds carrying twigs, bits of wool, moss, and grass (and roofing tiles and bricks) in their beaks. No, they're not on 'litter duty'! They're nest building.

Watch where they go to find the location of the nest.

WARNING!
Once you find it you must do your utmost not to disturb the birds. If you do, they may abandon the nest and their babies will starve to death! Always move quietly and slowly and keep a good distance. When it's time, you may well be rewarded with the fantastic sight of the 'fledgling' birds leaving the nest for the first time. (A bit like your first day at school, except you weren't in danger of being eaten by the local cat!)

Typical. She always has to go one better

Build a brush pile for birds

Birds love hopping around in 'brush' piles. Simply collect fallen twigs and branches, then choose a corner of your garden that is popular with birds as a site for your synthetic thicket. Build it by criss-crossing a couple of layers of larger branches then tossing on smaller branches and twigs. Your brush pile will be alive with birds in no time!

I like your moustache

Drum-up a great spotted woodpecker

Woodpeckers 'drum' rapidly on trees and wooden posts with their beaks in order to attract mates and claim territory. The best time to try this activity is in March and April. Go into the woods and hit a tree trunk or log as fast as you can with a piece of wood. Having mistaken the noise for a rival trying to move in on its territory, a woodpecker may well begin drumming back at you.

Watch a greenfly infestation grow and grow. And be amazed!

Greenfly (aphids) live for just a few weeks. But in that time a single female produces millions, sometimes even *billions*, of descendants. Some species of aphids 'squirt out' a staggering 41 generations of children in a single summer!

Watch a wasp 'stealing' your garden furniture

Look for tell-tale 'scraped areas' on wooden garden furniture. If you're patient you'll see a wasp come and begin 'stealing' tiny amounts of your sun-lounger or patio table.

Track a wasp to its building site

If you can manage to follow one of these furniture-nibbling wasps you'll see that it's actually recycling the minute bits of wood it pinches by chewing them into a papery mush then turning the mush into an exquisite little nest. You often find these lovely creations hanging from the insides of shed roofs.

You'll make an excellent branch manager

Listen out for a 'yaffle'

Green woodpeckers were called 'yaffles' by old country people because of the mad laughing noise they make. If you're out in the fields and hear what you think is an escaped lunatic cackling insanely, it could well be a yaffle. You'll recognise them by their fabulous green feathers and 'big-dipper' flight style.

Investigate some yaffle poo

Yaffles really are flying anteaters. They spend much of the time on the ground digging into the nests then licking up dozens of ants with their really long tongues. If you ever find a green woodpecker's dropping and break it open you'll discover that it's often entirely made up of the remains of ants.

On the web

Listen to yaffles on the internet. There are loads of other bird calls on there too.

www.RSPB.org.uk/wildlife/birdguide/nature/g/greenwoodpecker/

Examine a bird's wing

You can learn about birds' bodies simply by studying a chicken bought from a supermarket (and when you're tired of studying, you can eat it). Once you've got your chicken, 'study' with it. For instance, manipulate its legs and wings to see how they're attached to the main body and how they move. Then, once you've got an overall feel for the 'design' of your chicken, it's time to study one part in particular: the wing. Get your grown-up to cut one of the wings off and boil it until the skin and meat have gone soft. Let it cool then pull as much of the skin and meat off the bones as you can. Don't throw all the meat away – give it back to your adult for when they're preparing dinner. Now ask them to boil the bones a second time before scrubbing them with an old toothbrush to get them really 'clean'. Lay out the bones for identification and labelling. You'll see that the wing is rather like a human arm.

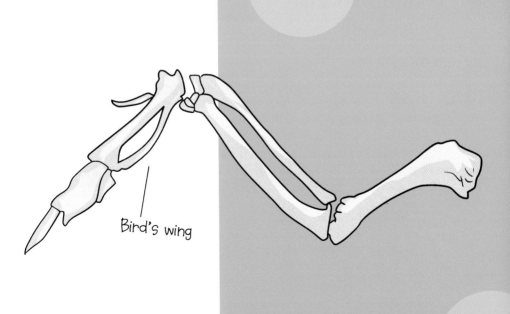

Bird's wing

Get to grips with geotropism

Despite what most people think, plants are incredibly brainy and ... well, sensitive actually! On planet Earth, their roots always grow downwards because they sense gravity. But in outer space, that's not the case, as you'll discover by carrying out the next few activities. A tropism is something that happens when a plant reacts to a stimulus. Geotropism is a plant's natural reaction to gravity. It ensures that the plant thrusts its roots into life-giving soil (rather than just lying on its back and waggling them around in the air like a total twerp).

Prove that geotropism always works on planet Earth

WHAT YOU NEED:

- Some kitchen roll
- A bean
- A plastic bag with a seal
- Water
- A drawing pin
- A cork noticeboard

WHAT TO DO:

1. Soak the kitchen roll, fold it to fit in the bag, place the bean on it and then partly seal the bag so that some air can get in. Pin the bag to the board so that the bean stays in place.

2. When the bean throws out a root and a shoot, turn the bag the other way up and pin it to the board again.

3. Watch as the root reacts to gravity and turns to grow downwards while the shoot grows upwards.

4. Pin the bag in different positions and watch the pattern repeat itself.

Get familiar with Google Earth

Download Google Earth to your computer and be amazed by your home planet:

www.earth.google.com

See the miracle of phototropism taking place in fantastic HD-3D

Phototropism is a plant's reaction to sunlight. Grow a seedling in a plant pot on a windowsill and watch how the shoots grow in the direction of the light. Now swizzle the pot round and see how the seedling shoots twist to follow the source of light again.

Can we stop now? I feel sick.

And if you want to prove that geotropism doesn't work...

If you want to prove that geotropism doesn't work in zero gravity, gather together some basic spacecraft components, such as helicon double-layer thrusters, pyrotechnic valves, androgynous peripheral attachments and suchlike (available from all good DIY stores) and build yourself a rocket. When it's ready, launch yourself into space with the plastic bag, the wet kitchen roll, the corkboard and another, new bean. Once you've begun orbiting the earth, repeat experiment 244. You should now see that the plant no longer knows up from down and begins growing its roots and shoots every which way!

Wild Things To Do With Spiders

247 Keep a pet spider

Not all spiders spin webs. Plus catching live flies isn't easy…

WHAT TO DO:

Catch your spider and put it in your tegenarium (a posh name for a spider house). Feed it with the flies and creepy crawlies. Watch to see if it spins a web (and frightens little girls sitting on tuffets).

Do you mind? I'm just having my lunch.

248 Set up some web sites for your local spiders

The easiest way to do this is by hanging old picture frames around your garden. You can also make web sites by hanging wire coat hangers on tree branches. Being so compulsively creative and industrious, spiders just won't be able to resist the challenge and soon your web sites will contain silken masterpieces.

Collect a genuine and completely original work of spider art

On a really still day, have a wander round until you find a real humdinger of a spider's web. Make sure no one is at home, taking particular care to check the edges of the web and any nooks and crannies where the spider might be curled up sleeping off last night's bluebottle. When you're sure the web is spider-free, hold a sheet of paper behind it and gently squirt your spray paint on it. Do this on both sides of the web. Don't get too close, or you'll just blast the web to smithereens. Let the paint dry for a few minutes then spray your web with hairspray until it's sticky. **BTW**: If at this point the spider returns to its web, you're going to have a lot of explaining to do!

Now, before the hairspray dries, take your piece of card, position it so that it's perfectly in line with the web and the entire web is not larger than the piece of card. Then, with one smooth, seamless and supremely confident movement, press it against the web so that the whole thing sticks to it. Finally, cut the web away from whatever it was attached to and, having given your little treasure a final blast of sticky spray, mount it in a frame and hang it on your wall.

WHAT YOU NEED:
- A piece of card
- A piece of paper
- Spray paint
- Hairspray

How inspiring

Wild Things To Do With Spiders

Get tickled by baby spiders' 'parachutes'

If you walk out on an autumn morning, you may well feel several strands of spider silk tickling your face, then notice that tiny spiders are attached to them and wonder, 'However did they get up here? Surely they can't be flying'. And they're not! The tiny baby spiders, often known as spiderlings, aren't actually flying, they're doing what is known as 'ballooning'. When spiderlings want to flit off and seek their fortune, they simply shoot a few strands of gossamer silk out of their back end to make a triangular 'parachute', wait for the breeze to catch it, then they're up and away. Some rides end just a short distance away, but others go on for miles. Some 'long-haul' ballooning spiders have been spotted by aircraft pilots and others have been discovered hundreds of miles from land, having landed on ships' sails.

Weeeeeeeee!

251 Send a spider 'ballooning'

Gently encourage a tiny spiderling or money spider to climb onto your finger tip. Blow on it and watch it shoot out its silken parachute and go 'cruising'.

252 Make a spider ladder for your bath

When spiders fall into the bath, the poor little arachnids can't get out again because they're unable to climb the slippery sides. Save them from dying of starvation (or from going completely mad) by making a spider ladder. Simply dangle some twine (or cut up nylon tights) from the taps so that they have something to climb up. (Or, failing that, line the bottom of your bath with high quality trampoline elastic.)

Watch some water lice

Water lice are crustaceans and are closely related to woodlice (the main difference is that woodlice still haven't got their swimming badges). You can find them in wild ponds. Have a close look at them and you'll soon see the similarities! In fact, woodlice are one of the very few crustaceans that live on land. If you study one carefully you'll see that they actually still have gills for extracting oxygen from water. Now all you need to do is find some water lice and see for yourself.

Make a wildlife picture map using the Internet

You could make a wildlife map of your own garden, the local area, or somewhere you're taking a holiday. Once you've chosen the place and decided what points of interest you're going to feature, you can design your own symbols for things like trees, streams, buildings, flowers and animals (and haunted garden sheds). Don't forget to include a key so that people looking at your map are 100% sure what the symbols represent. You could include things on your map such as the location of birds' nests, the sandy bank where the rabbits like to burrow or the pond that's home to dragonflies, newts and frogs – whatever the wildlife highlights of your chosen area are!

Using your map, your friends will be able to take a safari around the area you've charted, knowing to be particularly quiet as they approach a spot where wildlife is likely to be.

Make plaster casts of wild animal tracks

This activity is a fun way of learning to recognise different animal tracks.

WHAT YOU NEED:
- A mixing bowl
- Some paperclips
- Scissors
- A spoon
- Plaster of Paris
- A jug
- Some cardboard

WHAT TO DO:

1. Go out and find some wild animal tracks in mud or wet sand. Snow won't work because the warm plaster will melt it before it has set. Tidy up the tracks by removing leaves, twigs and bits of earth.

2. Make a ring of cardboard big enough to encircle the track, and fasten it with the paperclips. Press it down into the earth around the tracks, making sure there are no gaps.

3. Mix your plaster with some warm water. Keep mixing and adding water until it has the consistency of single cream. Now pour it into the cardboard ring and wait for it to set (this should take about an hour).

4. When the plaster seems firm, carefully lift up the whole thing with the cardboard still attached. Now leave the plaster to set really hard (about 24 hours). When it's solid, remove the cardboard ring so that you can admire and display your track casts.

Send a flower two-tone

Plants suck up water through tiny veins in the roots and stems by a process called osmosis. With this activity you'll see just how it happens.

WHAT TO DO:

1. Fill the glasses with water and stir two or three drops of food colouring into one of them. Lay your flower on a board and get your grown-up to split its stem part way up using the sharp knife.

2. Tape the top of the cut to stop the stem splitting any further.

3. Put one half of the stem in one glass and one in the other. By now the flower may be feeling quite faint so give it something to lean against. The flower will now begin slurping. And you'll know when the water has reached its petals because half of them will change colour!

WHAT YOU NEED:

- A pale flower such as a white carnation or lily
- Two glasses or vases
- A sharp knife
- Sticky tape
- Some water
- Food colouring
- Your tame grown-up

Dear Dragonfly This is your life!

Draw the life cycle of a dragonfly.

Ditto butterfly

Draw the life cycle of a butterfly.

Find out just how 'thick-skinned' water is

You've no doubt now seen the whirligig beetles whirling crazily and pond skaters skating skilfully across the surface of the wildlife pond you built in activities 51–52. How on earth do they manage it? Here's a way to find out.

All you need is a bowl of water, some tweezers and a needle. Simply pick up the needle with the tweezers and lower it onto the surface of the water. Now gently open the tweezers and, hey presto, the needle will rest on the water's skin and not sink. Now waggle your fingers in the water and watch the needle sink. This isn't just useful for beetles and pond skaters – but also handy if you want to skim stones across a pond or lake! A skilful skimmer can make seriously slim stones serially skip across the surface.

Dinner?

'Obedience-train' your pet fish

Every time you feed your fish, whistle just before you put the food in the water. Or, if you can't whistle, ring a bell or give a short blast on one of those blower thingies you get at parties. Do this every day for a few weeks. In time, your fish will come to associate the sound with the idea of food and come to the surface every time they hear it. Or they might just decide that you're completely bonkers – try it and find out!

Make a fish print

Almost everything in nature is brilliantly designed and quite beautiful. But sometimes it's only when we study a plant or animal, or see it in unusual circumstances, that its true beauty strikes us. Fish prints were first made by Japanese fishermen as a way of recording their catch but now, 'gyotaku' or fish printing, is an art form which really brings out the beauty of fish.

WHAT YOU NEED:

- A fish from your local fishmonger
- newspaper
- Kitchen roll or a clean tea towel
- Acrylic paint
- A roller or paint brush
- An old baking tray
- A sheet of paper to print on

WHAT TO DO:

1. Rinse your fish then dry it with the tea towel or kitchen roll. Put a small amount of paint on the tray. Coat your roller or paint brush with paint.

2. Put the fish paint-side down on the paper. Press it gently, making sure that you include the parts that curve away from the paper. Lift the fish straight up and be amazed at your spectacular work-of-art. And when you're done with your fish, you could wash it and give it to your tame adult to fry with some chips!

I'm forever blowing bubbles! Expose a frog hopper

Have you ever noticed all those disgusting blobs of 'saliva' that appear in the garden in spring, making it look like a team of professional footballers have been wandering around and spitting for all they're worth? Actually, some people think another culprit is responsible for all the saliva and blame it on a visiting summer bird, calling it 'cuckoo' spit! Well, the guilty party is neither footballers nor cuckoos. It's the nymph of a little bug known as a common green frog hopper. The blobs of 'spit' are actually bubbles that it blasts out of its backside in order to hide itself from all the predators that want to eat it. If you gently stroke the bubbles away with a small paintbrush you'll eventually expose the frog hopper. But it won't stay exposed for long! It will soon be sucking the sap out of whatever plant it happens to be on and blasting out more bubbles, faster than a jacuzzi full of baked-bean addicts.

Find out what your local nature was like years ago

During the last fifty years, lots of Britain's native birds, plants and butterflies have either disappeared or had their numbers drastically reduced. But people who were children in the 1950s remember streams teeming with fish, meadows full of wildflowers and woods filled with drumming woodpeckers and screeching magpies. Talk to someone who was young then and get them to tell you about their personal wildlife experiences. Why not record their memories before they're lost for all time?

Experience the soft cell!

Just like all other living things, we're made up from masses of little building blocks called cells. Nobody is exactly sure how many cells make up a human but it is thought to be in the region of 100 trillion (and not a single one contains a prisoner). Our cells all have different jobs to do, such as enabling us to move, sensing our surroundings and helping us to think (no prizes for guessing where those cells are).

Experience the hard cell!

Plant cells are very inflexible: they don't bend and they've got a tough outer wall, which gives them a fixed shape. This is really handy – big wobbly oak trees flopping this way and that like giant jellies would be extremely inconvenient, and dangerous! Some plant cells are much bigger than animal cells and you can actually see them with a magnifying glass. Get your adult to cut an onion in half then cut a small section from it. (No blubbing!) Peel a film-like sliver from it and press it on a window so that it sticks. Now you can look at its cells with a magnifying glass.

You can have fun making a model of a group of human cells. Fill a load of balloons with water then squidge them into a big fish tank as tightly as they'll go. Now pour water on them. The water represents the fluid that keeps cells alive in animals. If you give the 'balloon cells' a good squeeze you'll find that they're squishy and flexible just like most animal cells. If they were rigid and inflexible, like plant cells, we'd all end up completely stiff and unyielding.

Can everyone just be a little more flexible?

Find out if it's really there

You can't see it and a lot of the time you can't even feel it, but it's all around us and without it we'd die! What is it? It's air! And along with other things such as nitrogen, water, carbon dioxide and bacteria, it contains that magic ingredient, oxygen, which all animals depend on for survival. But if we can't see it, how can we prove it exists? Here's how: Put a funnel in a jar and firmly seal the join with plenty of modelling clay. Now pour some water into the funnel. If you've made your seal completely airtight, the water will fill the funnel but not the jar. Why? Because the jar is full of air which cannot get out. The air prevents the water getting in. Use a pencil to make a hole in the plasticine and you'll see the water pour into the jar as the air escapes.

Collect a bird's nest

When the breeding season is long over and the leaves have fallen from the trees, you'll no doubt spot birds' nests in trees and hedges. Perhaps you'll even say to yourself, "Well I never! I didn't for one moment suspect that a bird's nest was in that spot."

Birds are extremely clever at building and camouflaging their nests and in the summer, the only indication of their presence is the adult birds returning to the same spot with beaks full of food and the babies cheeping. A lot of people think birds' nests are just scruffy clumps of twigs leaves and mud. But they aren't. Each type of bird builds its own unique nest. For instance, long-tailed tits' nests are beautiful little balls built from moss, spiders' webs, lichen, feathers and hair; while kingfishers dig long tunnels in river banks for their nests; and house martins build mud cups under the eaves of houses. The Chinese were so impressed by the structure of birds' nests that they built their huge Olympic National Stadium in the shape of one!

Some birds use the same nests each year, so don't collect one of these. These nests tend to be built in high places and belong to birds such as herons, rooks, crows and birds of prey. You certainly wouldn't want to collect a golden eagle's nest, which is over 2 metres (2.19 yards) in diameter and incredibly heavy.

Also, don't remove the mud nests of swallows and house martins as they also tend to re-use their nests.

WHAT TO DO:

To remove a nest you'll need a pair of tough gloves to protect you from thorns, and secateurs to cut it free. Most birds firmly 'bind' their nests to twigs, so they're not always easy to remove. Once you've removed the nest, leave it to dry and then put it in plastic bag with some mothballs. This will kill any fleas, carpet beetles (or escaped prisoners) that may still be lurking inside. Your next job is to identify your nest using books or the internet.

After that you can do one of two things with your nest. You can either add it to your nature table display or take it to pieces with tweezers, in order to discover how it was made. But if you do this, don't forget to take photographs or make sketches at each stage of the dissection.

Spot boxing hares in March

It's thought that hares were first brought to Britain a long time ago by the Normans. In spring you can see the astonishing sight of 'mad March hares' boxing! They're not 'boxing' in the normal sense of the word. The female hares are actually doing their best to fend off 'overfriendly', love-starved male hares. If you aren't lucky enough to see this amazing sight for real, watch it on this fantastic video.

www.bbc.co.uk/nature/species/
European_Hare#p003b0qr

Grow a tomato in a bottle

Show people a ship in a bottle and they'll say, 'Ah, it's all done with hinges and tweezers!'. But show them a fully-grown tomato in a bottle and they might be completely baffled as to how it got there.

WHAT TO DO:

Choose a small, unripe tomato fruit on your plant. It must have a long stem and be small enough to go through the neck of your bottle, Gently push the fruit and stem down inside the bottle. Now loosely tie the bottle to a strong branch of your tomato plant using the twist ties or string. Make sure the bottle has a bit of shade – you don't want your tomato cooking in the hot sun! Once your tomato is completely ripe, snip the stem and take off all the ties. There's your tomato in a bottle!

WHAT YOU NEED:

- A tomato plant
- Twist ties or string
- A large, clear plastic bottle (light enough to tie to your tomato plant without damaging it, but big enough to hold a ripe tomato fruit)

Watch a plant produce some oxygen

270

Go to a pet shop or tropical fish shop and buy some Canadian pondweed (Elodea canadensis).

Canadian pondweed works extra hard to produce oxygen, so it's very popular with fish keepers. Put a small bunch of Canadian pondweed in the tank you set up in activity 118. Lower a glass jar into the tank and let it fill with water. Now put it upside-down over the pondweed. Leave the tank in a sunny spot and watch the oxygen bubbles coming off the pondweed and collecting at the top of the jar.

WARNING!

Never put your pondweed back in a pond.

Go on a wasp garden safari

Most people think of wasps as those flying insects wearing yellow-and-black stripy rugby shirts and landing on your ice cream. However, there are hundreds of other sorts of wasps in Britain. One of them is extremely small, and goes by the scientific name of 'Dinocampus coccinellae'.

This little wasp makes the stripey wasps look like fluffy bunnies! When a mother Coccinellae is ready to lay an egg, she finds a ladybird and lays the egg inside it! Then the little wasp hatches as a larva and eats the living ladybird's insides. Next, it bites the ladybird's leg nerves in order to paralyse it. It then weaves itself a cocoon between the ladybird's legs.

The ladybird eventually starves to death, but by then the adult Coccinellae has hatched from its cocoon and is already looking for a mate and a ladybird to lay its own eggs in.

Check out how fast your fingernails grow

Dab a little spot of nail varnish on the bottom part of one of your fingernails. See how long it takes to reach the top, as your nail grows.

Draw the life cycle of a frog

Or even a frog on a cycle!

Splat! Check out a very fascinating, but gruesome, scenario

In summer days the air is alive with insects flitting this way and that. No doubt they're thinking: What a lovely day. Oh, I get such a buzz out of being a bee! But then, just when they're thinking things can't get any better, a motorist ends their carefree existence!

Splat! Millions of insects are squidged by cars every day, ending up stuck to radiator grills, bonnets and windscreens. But if you're fascinated by bugs, their bad luck is *your* good luck! And if you want to hugely increase the amount of insects you 'bag', put some double-sided sticky tape on your family car's bumpers. Examine the car after a journey and you'll be amazed at the variety and number of glorious insects stuck to it. And some of them will be in remarkably good condition!

Uh oh!

Get low down and dirty

When you're really small, you're very aware of all the interesting things going on near the surface of the earth. However, as people get older, and taller, they literally 'lose touch' with all of that.

Which is perhaps why so many adults miss out on all the fascinating and wonderful stuff that exists below knee level. One way to almost become part of the living earth is simply by lying down in a spot that's busy with mini-beasts, maybe in leaf litter of the forest floor, some long grass or a path next to a flower bed or hedge bottom, then observing all the drama and action taking place down there.

After a while, you'll 'tune in' to this miniature world in which columns of ants march this way and that, spiders feast on flies and weird-looking creepy crawlies slither, squirm and do battle. So strange is this tiny kingdom that you might soon find yourself thinking you're on the surface of an another planet.

And if you don't fancy doing the lying down bit, why not just crawl round on your hands and knees for a while? You might spot some ladybirds munching greenfly or a colourful caterpillar spinning a chrysalis.

276

Bring a little bud to life

As everyone knows, many trees lose their leaves in the autumn. However, even as that's happening, new leaves are beginning to develop inside buds in preparation for the coming spring. When spring finally arrives, snip off some twigs with buds that are beginning to swell. Bring them indoors and put them in a jar of water in a sunny spot. Watch how their outer scales unfold to reveal their glorious newborn leaves.

277

Make a simple underwater viewer

Often, when you look in ponds or rock pools to discover what fascinating little treasures are lurking in their depths, your view is spoiled – either by ripples or reflections on the surface. With this clever device you'll be able to see the comings and goings of all sorts of aquatic creatures quite clearly.

WHAT YOU NEED:
- A length of plastic drainage pipe (with a broad diameter)
- Really tough, 'heavy-duty' clingfilm
- Sticky tape/duct tape (the stronger and stickier the better)

Some kind of undiscovered species, I think

Visit a nature reserve near you

For a really wild day out, see pages 186-187 for further information.

On the web

The Big Garden Bird Watch always takes place in January because the cold weather always brings birds into our gardens, looking for food and shelter, so it's the best time of the year for watching garden birds. All you do is count and list the birds you see for one hour. You choose which hour, on the designated day. Lots more info at this web link

www.rspb.org.uk/birdwatch

WHAT TO DO:

1. Stretch the clingfilm over one end of your plastic pipe, making sure it comes quite a long way up the side. Use your sticky tape to securely fasten the cling film to the outside of the pipe.

2. Go to a pond or rock pool and lower the end of the pipe covered in cling-film into the water. Now look through the other end and be mesmerised by all the previously unseen underwater marvels.

List all the autumn fruits in your garden and local countryside

You'll probably spot crab apples which some people use to make jelly, the deep crimson fruits of wild roses known as rosehips, juicy blackberries, blue-black sloes, red hawthorn berries and bright scarlet rowan berries. They all make brilliant subjects for wildlife photos and sketches.

On the web

Visit the Natural History Museum

www.nhm.ac.uk

Identify an insect using Internet 'keys'

If you're out lifting up logs and sifting through soil you're bound to turn up all sorts of intriguing little wrigglers. But what if you're completely clueless as to what they are?

Er... I think it's a pond skater

Or a squirrel

As an alternative to leafing through books to identify your finds, you can go on the internet and use the really helpful 'keys' that help you find out what you've got. Answer the questions that refer to things like how many wings has your insect got, whether it has got pincers (or spotty fur). Then, through what is known as a process of elimination, the key will lead you to what is most likely your insect, which you can compare with a photograph. Of course, you may find an insect that is completely unidentifiable. In which case, you can claim it as a newly discovered species and have it named after yourself!

Join a Nature Club

The RSPB run a nature club, called RSPB Wildlife Explorers: www.rspb.org.uk/youth/join_in/wex.asp

You could also investigate whether there is a local Nature Club for your area.

On the web

Get inspired by this great nature-sketching site http://naturesketchers.blogspot.com/

285 On the web

A couple of really useful insect 'key' sites are:

www.nhm.ac.uk/nature-online/life/insects-spiders/

www.amentsoc.org/insects/what-bug-is-this/adult-key.html

286 Test the weather 'experts'

Check out the weather forecasts on the internet, TV and radio and observe how accurate they turn out to be.

Use the internet to research wild places to visit

Discover all the best really wild places to visit on pages 186–187 at the back of this book.

287 On the web

Go on the internet and reassemble a virtual squirrel skeleton. Here's where to do it:

http://www.kidwings.com/skulls/redsquirrel/index.htm

288 Make a collection of dried grasses

Dried grasses look magnificent arranged in a vase. There are dozens of different sorts to collect including quaking grass with its lovely lantern-like flowers, common reedmace, which many people mistakenly call bullrush, wild oats, cotton grass, cockspur, meadow foxtail and Yorkshire fog.

Put together your own nature table

You can put all sorts of fabulous finds on your nature table including dried leaves, small branches or twigs, acorns, walnuts, almonds, shells, stones, flowers, feathers, or even a dead spider or dragonfly. Keeping an eye open for things for your nature table will make walks in the countryside twice as exciting and challenging.

Put together your own 'natural history museum'

All sorts of things can go in your museum, maybe a disused wasps' nest, tiny animal bones, or plaster casts of wild tracks or feathers.

Sketch a plant

Sketch without picking if possible, and try to get close up. You'll see all sorts of hairy stems, or maybe tiny creatures lurking if you're lucky.

On the web

Download some nature screen savers or wallpapers for your computer.

www.screene.com/free-screensavers/nature-screensavers/

Let colour and patterns in nature inspire you!

You can make designs and abstract art by looking at the natural world. Let your imagination go wild!

Take wildlife photos and collect your top shots

You can save your fabulous photos electronically on your computer or print them out for an album.

Listen out for the KERPOW! of exploding seed pods in summer

If you're out in the countryside or in your garden on a warm day in summer you may well hear lots of little 'snapping' sounds. This is the noise that the pods of certain types of seed make when they explode, hurling their seeds through the air so that they fall on fresh places to grow.

Preserve leaves in all their autumn glory

You can preserve leaves and retain their fabulous colours by using glycerin (you can buy it in chemists and in the home-baking area of supermarkets). You'll get the best results if you pick the leaves just as they're changing colour.

WHAT TO DO:

1. Add 2 parts boiling water to 1 part glycerin and mix them together. Once the mixture's cooled a bit, pour it into a jar and put the leaf in the warm glycerin solution so that just its stem is submerged. The leaf will slurp up the glycerin in the same way it slurped sap from its tree. You'll know when it has had enough because drops of glycerin will appear on the surface of the leaf.

2. Now remove your leaf from the solution and wipe off the glycerin drops. When you've done a good variety of leaves put them on thick stacks of newspaper for a few days to dry out, then wash them gently with a little soap and water.

3. Finally, peg them on a line to dry before displaying them. Note! Don't use leaves that have already fallen from their trees because they're dead (and couldn't absorb the glycerin even if they wanted to).

Go fossil-hunting

There are lots of places where eagle-eyed young naturalists can find fossils. Check out internet sites like this one for their locations:

www.ukfossils.co.uk/news_new.htm

Turn your wildlife photos into a slide show

Once you've put your slide show together why not invite your friends for a special viewing and accompany the slides with your recordings of natural sounds.

Write your name on a pumpkin and watch it grow

Plant a pumpkin seed and when a small pumpkin finally appears, scratch your name on it and watch your name grow as the pumpkin grows.

Take macro photos of mosses and lichens

When you look at them, you might think you're getting a bird's eye view of a rainforest!

Check out some human eyelash mites

Humans have tiny arachnids called mites, which are about 0.3 to 0.4 mm long, living on their eyelashes. They eat skin flakes and natural oil from the skin, which is called sebum. To look at mites you'll need a microscope. Remove one of your eyelashes or eyebrow hairs, put it under the microscope, and look for eyelash mites. Now remove an eyelash from your tame adult and study that, too. Who had the most mites?

Check out some bumblebee mites

Bumblebees also have mites (but not on their eyelashes). Some bumblebees have so many mites clinging to them that the weight of their cheeky little hitchhikers actually stops them flying or causes them to wobble all over the place as they flit from flower to flower. Carefully study the bees that are pollinating flowers to see if they have any mites. But remember: female bumblebees can sting if you upset them – so, *don't* tease your bees!

Make a rainbow using a glass

Put a glass of water next to a sunny window. Where the sun passes through the glass, look for a rainbow!

Sprout some potatoes

In the spring, put some potatoes in an egg carton and leave them out in a light position at room temperature for a few weeks. After a while, the spuds will produce little green shoots. This is called 'chitting' and it's what gardeners do before they plant potatoes.

Make a potato maze

Put one of your 'chitted' spuds in a small plant pot filled with damp potting compost. Now stand a shoe box on end and put the pot in the left-hand corner of shoebox. Make a hole at the top right-hand corner of the shoebox. Loosely fill the box with obstacles such as plastic blocks, cotton reels and lightweight balls to create the maze. Mind you don't knock the growing shoot.

Alternatively, you can create the 'maze' from strips of card glued to the box. Put the lid back on the box and place it with the hole facing the light. Mr Potato will now be desperate to send his shoot to the light source. But what with all those obstacles in the way, will he make it? Check his progress every few days, remembering to dampen his compost if it dries out.

That was easy!

Go walking on a windy day for fun!

The Dutch do it all the time. And they even have a word for it … Uitwaaien!

You know it makes scents!

Go sniffing on a warm, wet spring day. Try to describe all the different smells you sniffed and work out where they came from.

Learn the Latin names of ten natural things

All over the world, people have their own local names for plants and animals. In order to sort things out a bit, scientists decided to give them scientific names, which could be recognised by naturalists throughout the world. For example, they called the common toad, *Bufo bufo*, the wren, *Troglodytes troglodytes* and the bumblebee, *Bombus pascuorum*. Look up ten scientific names for animals and plants and see if you can memorise them.

Leave no stone unturned (or log, or old piece of carpet for that matter)

This is a great way to uncover a hundred and one wild creatures. But remember to replace them afterwards!

Bamboozle some butterflies

Attach a butterfly-sized piece of white cloth or butterfly-shaped white card to a length of wire (a straightened-out coat hanger works well) then waggle it around where white butterflies are flying. Mistaking it for a beautiful lady butterfly, male butterflies will come to check out the action. They'll be disappointed by your decoy, but you'll get a great view of the butterflies up close in the process.

Find out how fast you grow

Attach a measuring chart to your bedroom wall and mark the height and date every few weeks.

More bamboozling!

You can do the same trick with coloured butterflies by using coloured decoys.

Go on a city safari

Take your tame adult for a wander around a city centre and make a list of all the wild things you see.

Despite all those choking traffic fumes, crowds and noise you'll be surprised at what you discover. Cities are homes to all sort of wildlife including familes of foxes and mice, birds of prey, gulls and wildflowers. If all the humans left a city for six months nature would reclaim it in no time!

Make a rock collection

A lot of people don't give much thought to the stuff we walk around on, but once you start to investigate all the various types of rock our planet is made up of, you'll never look at a coin, a stone wall, a pencil or a cliff face in the same way again! To kick off your collection, simply collect 10 stones of different shapes, sizes and colours. Once you've assembled them, use the internet to identify what sort of rocks they are and how they came to be here in the first place. You'll soon realise that the ground beneath our feet is changing constantly and that even the most ordinary looking chunk of stone has the most extraordinary life story.

Read *Tarka the Otter* by Henry Williamson

Read this brilliant tale of an otter cub who loses his family when his home is attacked by otter hunters.

Make a 'jungle' in a bottle

Fill the bottom of a large glass jar with a layer of gravel with a bit of charcoal mixed in. Now add a second layer: one-third soil, one-third sand and one-third compost. Plant your bottle jungle with small plants. Choose plants that don't grow too big, too fast or drop too many leaves or petals. Slip them into the bottle through a paper tube and firm them in with a cotton reel or piece of cork attached to a stick.

Now water your jungle gently, seal it and leave in a light place (but not in direct sun.) After a week or so, don't be surprised to see several tiny Tarzans wandering around in there!

FASCINATING FACT!

The total weight of insects on our planet is more than that of all other species put together. (There are some really fat insects out there.)

Who are you calling fat?

Use your family camcorder as a microscope

Camcorders have all sorts of snazzy facilities including zoom and macro (close-up) lenses. Experiment with them to investigate, film and photograph mini-beasts, insects and wild flowers. Tip! Your images will look loads better if you mount your camcorder on a tripod. Even with a really steady hand, the slightest tremble is magnified by the 'macro' mode.

Wild Things To Do With Trees

Make a cone collection (tree, not traffic)

Some trees don't have fruit or flowers, but produce their seeds inside cones.

If you go for walk in a 'coniferous woodland' with trees such as pines, firs and spruces, it's fun to collect their various cones. When you get home you can display and label your collection. Also, if the cones are closed, watch for their scales opening in warm dry weather. If you look inside, you'll see their seeds with paper-like wings.

Pull a seed out with tweezers, let it go and watch it spiral to the floor. On windy days these spinning seeds are blown all over the place, ensuring that at least a few of them take root to create new trees.

Buy a Christmas tree with roots

That way you won't have to make it yet another wasteful society 'throw-away'! And in the New Year you can plant it outside, festooned with bird food.

You could always adopt a tree in your garden and decorate that instead!

Plant a tree

If you search the area surrounding mature trees like chestnuts, oak and ash, you'll find little saplings growing. Dig one up, put it in a big plant pot filled with compost and watch it grow.

WILD THINGS TO DO WITH WOODLICE

On the web
Learn to tell the difference between deciduous and coniferous trees.
www.woodlandtrust.org.uk

Photograph and list all the trees in your local area
You can make a list, and stick your pics in below.

_____

_____

_____

_____

_____

_____

_____

_____

Stick your photos here

Watch leaves change colour in October

During a few weeks in Autumn, the green leaves of deciduous trees give themselves a fabulous makeover turning red, orange, yellow, gold, brown and all the shades in between. It's stunning … don't miss it!

Put a bird identification book on your Christmas wish list

Then spend hours of fun outside trying to spot all the different types.

Watch birds migrating in September

In the Autumn flocks of British summer bird visitors gather to make their way back south for warmer climates. But as *they're* departing, new birds begin to arrive here including fieldfares, redwings and different sorts of swans, geese and wading birds.

Watch out for new bird arrivals in spring

When the warm weather comes in April and May, the first of millions of visiting summer birds begin to arrive in Britain. Most of them fly here all the way from Africa, covering vast distances, navigating their way through storms, over deserts, rainforests and oceans. And not only do they manage to get here in one piece but they also mate and bring up broods of chicks before whole families fly back to Africa for the winter. So watch and listen out for high flying swifts, swallows swooping in pursuit of insects, willow warblers and chiffchaffs filling gardens and woods with song, and of course, the familiar, but increasingly rare, call of cuckoos as they seek out other birds' nests to lay their eggs.

Sniff out wild garlic

Wild garlic, also known as ramsons, grows in deciduous woodland and flowers in the spring, filling the air with a *very* garlicy smell.

Make an abode for a toad

All you need is an old clay flowerpot and a hidden corner of the garden.

Get in touch with your artistic nature

Photograph nature then make paintings and drawings from your photographs.

Visit an otter sanctuary

Otters are absolutely brilliant to watch! They're inquisitive, intelligent and playful and you'll be delighted to see them sliding down muddy banks, chasing and wrestling playfully. They're fantastic divers and swimmers too. Here's a link to a list of sanctuaries to visit:

www.amblonyx.com/otter.php?id=PlacesIndex

Learn bird song through handy memory aids known as mnemonics

For instance the frightened blackbird sounds like it's shouting pink! pink! pink!, a great tit appears to be calling tea-cher, tea-cher, tea-cher and a robin makes a tic tic noise.

Match these old country names for wild animals to the modern ones

OLD:

throstle cock; pollywiggler; doodlebug; wind hover; cherry chopper; dumbledore; flittermouse; bog jumper; weasel coot.

NEW:

bumblebee; bat; kestrel; tadpole etc. See if you can find the rest!

Look for wood ants sunbathing in February

After the long cold winter, wood ants 'sunbathe' on heaps of pine needles, absorbing the energy-giving warmth of the early spring sunshine!

Become a phenologist!

It's easier than you think. Simply observe events in the lives of plants and animals and record how they're affected by the seasons and changes in the weather.

Visit a bluebell wood in April or May

Drink in the glorious scent and listen for the first cuckoo of spring. Heaven!

Look out for new molehills in April

The biggest one will usually be situated just above the main 'football-sized' nest which is known as the 'fortress'.

338 Shake it about

Shake some seeds from a poppy head in June.

342 On the web

Check out Charles Darwin:

www.darwin200.org

339 Watch flying ants!

On certain warm days in mid-summer, huge swarms of winged black ants take to the skies and begin to mate like there's no tomorrow. And for many of them, there isn't! Some mate while they're flying, while others mate in trees and on rooftops. After the party, the ants lose their wings, or just bite them off.

Solve these tree anagrams

koa; owlwil; stunchet; macyrose; mel; borneham

Tree anagrams answers:
oak; willow; chestnut; sycamore; elm; hornbeam

341 Find out about the naturalist 'Grey Owl'

Grey Owl (1888–1938) was a wise native American Indian who knew all about nature and wilderness survival because he was brought up in the woods. Or so everyone thought!

343 Build a nesting raft for some ducks
And keep their ducklings safe from foxes!

You'll need your grown-up to help with this. It needs to float with its deck just above the water line. Don't forget to anchor it and add a ramp so that the ducklings can get in and out of the water easily.

344 Spot orange-tip butterflies in April
It's only the males of these small white butterflies that have the bright orange tips on their wings. They're there to warn birds that they taste horrid, mainly because of the mustard plants they like to eat. You'll see them flitting around meadows, hedgerows, gardens and the edges of woodland on the first warm days of spring.

345 Watch out for the first brimstone butterflies in March
These sulphur yellow beauties are usually the first butterflies you'll see in spring. You might even spot them in February if warm sun wakes them from their five month winter hibernation. Brimstone is the old name for sulphur.

Time travel 20,000 years into the past!

Go somewhere where there's absolutely no evidence of the existence of human beings (apart from you). Get a feel of what the world was like before we arrived!

Get enraptured by some raptors

You no longer need to be bored on those long car journeys. Instead gaze out of the window and be gobsmacked by the awesome site of dozens of magnificent birds of prey. Make a note of what you see in different areas. You'll get to where you're going in no time!

Slice a hyacinth bulb

Bulbs are 'soon-to-be' plants in a little package. They contain the complete plant in miniature, along with some food. If you get your grown-up to slice a bulb in half vertically, you'll see fleshy scales containing the food, immature leaves and the 'basal plate', from which the roots will eventually emerge.

Grow a hyacinth bulb

Put a single hyacinth bulb in a 'bulb glass' filled with water. Place it in the neck of the glass, so the water reaches a point just below the base of the bulb. The narrow neck of your bulb glass supports the bulb so that it remains dry while sending its roots down into the water. Place it in a well-ventilated, cool, dark place until its top growth reaches about 10 cm (4 inches). This should take between eight and ten weeks. Now bring the hyacinth into a room, but don't give it too much light at first. Get a worm's eye view of the roots while the leaves grow and the bulb flowers.

Download a birdsong ringtone for your mobile

Let a trilling wren, singing blackbird or calling thrush alert you to your incoming calls.

www.voeveo.co.uk/audio/ringtones/birds

Enter the Wildlife Explorer writing competition

Go wild with words! Join and find out more at:

www.rspb.org.uk/youth/join_in/wildlifeclub/club.asp

Enter WildPix, the RSPB Wildlife Explorers photographic competition

Get snap happy! More details can be found on the RSPB website. www.rspb.org.uk

Go on the internet and look at a live nature webcam

www.rspb.org.uk/webcams

Disturb a Devil's Coach Horse (if you dare!)

Devil's coach horses are big, black, scary-looking beetles which lurk in houses, sheds, gardens, parks and hedgerows. If you upset a devil's coach horse, it opens up its large, powerful jaws and raises up its rear end in a very menacing and scorpion-like manner. Beware! Not only do devil's coach horses squirt out disgusting smelly liquid from their backsides, but they can also give you a painful bite with those pincer-like jaws! They prey on woodlice and worms, eating the worms' insides to leave only the empty skin. In the old days, farm workers would put the body of a devil's coach horse beetle inside the handle of their scythes, as they believed it improved their crop-cutting skills.

Find out about the Reverend Gilbert White

Gilbert White (1720-1793) was one of the first people to write about wildlife and remind people that we should respect and look after the natural world.

He also wrote about his pet tortoise which he had 'inherited' from his Aunty.

On the web
Do a virtual pond dip at this web link:

http://microscopy-uk.org.uk/index.html

http://microscopy-uk.org.uk/ponddip/index.html

Come on! Want some do yer?

Expand and crop your nature photographs

When you zoom right it, you'll reveal some stunning natural designs which can be used for collages and other arty projects.

'Write' your name on a tomato

As well as growing tomatoes in a bottle, you can 'write' your name on them. Get a full-size tomato that is still green, cut out the letters of your name from plastic tape and stick them onto its skin. As it ripens, the skin underneath the tape, which isn't getting any sunlight, will remain green. When you peel the tape from the red tomato, you'll see your name 'in lights'!

Watch Internet videos of starlings doing synchronised swooping

On chilly winter evenings, after a hard day's feeding, starlings like nothing better than having a huge get-together. So, in places all over Britain, groups of starlings, some of which have been feeding as far as 20 miles (32 km) away from their roosting place, congregate above the spot where they're intending to spend the night. Then, for some reason best known to the starlings, thousands of them perform a spectacular series of superbly synchronised swoops, soars and swirls! A lot of people have commented on the fact that the assembled starlings look just like a single huge black creature with a mind of its own, rather than thousands of individuals. Search for videos online and see what you think.

www.youtube.com/watch?v=XH-groCeKbE

On the web

Go to this Internet site and discover how your lifestyle affects the environment:

www.footprint.wwf.org.uk/

Do your bit for nature!

List 10 things you and your family can do to improve the natural environment and then *do* them.

Magnified moss madness

Look at mosses and lichens through your handviewer. It's like a jungle in there!

Lure some bats with a paper hanky

Look out for broken eggshells in the summer

If you keep your eyes skinned in the summer, you'll seen broken egg shells in gardens and in the countryside. Some of these are birds' eggs that have been stolen by predators, such as jackdaws or foxes. Others are simply baby bird egg shells which have been removed from the nest by their very tidy parents.

Go out on a warm summer's evening when bats are flitting around and wave a paper hanky above your head. The curious creatures will swoop low to investigate the commotion. But don't worry, they won't swoop so low that they actually crash into you!

Take this nutty nature quiz

1. A grey plover is
   a) a rather boring item of knitwear
   b) a long-legged grey bird which visits Britain's coasts in the winter
   c) a long-legged grey bird closely related to the grey squirrel

2. A chrysalis is
   a) a type of large American car
   b) the stage in a butterfly's life just before it turns into a frog
   c) the pupal stage in a butterfly's life when its final metamorphosis occurs

3. A carnivore is
   a) an animal which eats meat
   b) an animal which eats cars
   c) someone who talks endlessly about cars

4. A parasite is
   a) somewhere safe for parachutists to land
   b) an animal or plant which lives on another animal or plant taking food from it but not killing it
   c) a heavenly place

5. A fen is
   a) someone who's really keen on something or someone
   b) low flat swampy land
   c) something to cool yourself with

6. The proper name for a daddy-long-legs is
   a) a crane fly
   b) a forklift truck fly
   c) a tractor fly

7. Is a catkin
   a) a really enormous kitten
   b) a dry oblong dangling flower spike
   c) a dry oblong dangling cat

8. An itchyologist is someone who
   a) studies fish
   b) studies ancient remains
   c) ought to take more baths

9. If a wild creature is most active at night it's said to be
   a) nocturnal
   b) diurnal
   c) dodgy

10. Is diversity
   a) an underwater town
   b) a Welsh university
   c) a wide range of variation in plants and animals

11. Is a frond
   a) a really good companion
   b) a pond reserved for frogs only
   c) part of a fern

12. A lepidopterist
   a) someone who studies leopards
   b) someone who studies moths and butterflies
   c) someone who studies lepids

13. The waggly things on ant's heads are known as
   a) antennae
   b) antlers
   c) fashion

14. Wild rabbits live in
   a) constant terror
   b) hare-conditioned apartments
   c) warrens

15. A young swan is known as
   a) a swanlet
   b) a cygnet
   c) a cigarette

Answers:
1. b, 2. c, 3. a, 4. b, 5. b, 6. a, 7. b, 8. b, 9. a, 10. c, 11. c, 12. b, 13. a, 14. c, 15. b

Further information

The RSPB speaks out for birds and wildlife, tackling the problems that threaten our environment. Nature is amazing – help us keep it that way. Find out more at:
www.rspb.org.uk

Find out more about RSPB Wildlife Explorers and how to become a member at:
www.rspb.org.uk/youth

Get involved

The RSPB runs many exciting campaigns and activities that you too can get involved in. Check them out at:
www.rspb.org.uk/thingstodo/surveys/

Other websites

The Wildlife Trusts (including Wildlife Watch)
www.wildlifetrusts.org.uk

BBC Science and Nature (including Springwatch, Autumnwatch and advice on garden wildlife)
www.bbc.co.uk/nature/animals/wildbritain

Wildfowl and Wetlands Trust
www.wwt.org.uk

British Butterfly Conservation
www.butterfly-conservation.org

UK Moths
www.ukmoths.org.uk

Wildlife Britain
www.wildlifebritain.com

Wildlife gardener.co.uk
www.wildlifegardener.co.uk

UK Department of the Environment (lots of information and activities to do with climate change)
www.defra.gov.uk/schools

WWF UK (information on wildlife and conservation at home and around the world)
www.wwf.org.uk

Wild places to visit

Check out these wildlife reserves in your local area
www.rspb.org.uk/reserves/area/

www.wwt.org/visit-us

www.wildlifetrust.org/index.php?section=localtrusts

www.woodlandtrust.org.uk/en/our-woods

Natural History Museum
www.nhm.ac.uk

Books

RSPB Guide to Birdwatching, Mike Unwin and David Chandler, A&C Black 2005

All About Garden Wildlife, David Chandler. New Holland, 2008

Collins Gem Garden Wildlife, Michael Chinery, Collins, 2006

Nick Baker's Bug Book, Nick Baker, New Holland, 2002

RSPB Where to Discover Nature in Britain and Northern Ireland, Marianne Taylor, A&C Black, 2009

RSPB Gardening For Wildlife, Adrian Thomas, A&C Black, 2010

Glossary

bacteria – tiny, one-celled organisms that are found in all living things. They normally live off other creatures or plants.

bait – food used to attract fish.

camouflaged – when something is hidden because it looks very similar to its surroundings, so blends into the background.

cirrus – a type of cloud; white and wispy.

compost heap – a collection of organic matter, such as bits of leftover food, left to decay. It will then turn into compost that can be used for growing and fertilising plants.

coniferous – evergreen, cone-bearing trees.

crustaceans – aquatic animals usually covered with a shell, such as crabs and lobsters.

cumulus – a type of cloud; fluffy and arranged in puffs/piles.

daphnia – known as 'water fleas', these are tiny crustaceans.

dawn chorus – birdsong at day break.

fungi – mushrooms and toadstools.

galaxy – a vast number of star systems held together by gravity, usually in a spiral shape.

geotropism – the downwards growth of a plant's roots, in response to gravity.

glycerin – a colourless, sweet liquid that can be used for preserving objects such as leaves.

growth rings – a series of rings inside a tree's trunk that show how old it is. A new ring is added every year.

honeydew – a sugary substance produced by greenfly. (Basically, it's greenfly poo!)

larvae – the newly hatched young of insects such as butterflies. They look very different from the adult form.

macro – very close-up photography.

mealworms – a type of beetle larva that are often used as bird feed.

metamorphosis – a complete change in form or structure.

microhabitat – any kind of habitat on a very small scale.

migrating – going from one country or region to another. For example, many birds migrate each year.

mites – very small creatures that are often parasitic.

molluscs – a type of invertebrate with a soft, unsegmented body. They usually have a shell.

moult – to shed hair, skin or feathers.

nymphs – the young of animals that undergo complete change (metamorphosis).

parasite – an animal or plant that lives in or on another (host) animal or plant, from which it obtains nourishment.

pellet – a small round lump that is regurgitated by birds such as owls, containing the indigestible bits of their prey.

phototropism – the growth of a plant's shoots towards sunlight.

pupae – insects in the stage between larva and metamorphosis (change) to the adult form. They are normally encased in a chrysalis or cocoon to protect them.

quadrat – four pieces of wood or plastic tubing fixed together to form a square. It can be placed on the ground to mark a particular spot.

predators – animals that eat other animals.

rain gauge – a device used to measure the amount of rainfall.

recycling – using again.

resolution – the sharpness (quality) of an image.

sap – the juice of a plant.

springwood – the light coloured section of a tree's growth rings.

stratus – a type of cloud; layers of flat, unbroken sheets.

summerwood – the dark coloured section of a tree's growth rings.

Tullgren funnel – a type of funnel with a sieve, used for removing small animals from leaves or soil.

venom – poison produced by animals.

zoom – make something far away appear close up in photography.

Index